MOVING TO DISCOVER THE USA

MIKE LEE
Small World Press

RHONDA L. CLEMENTS
Hofstra University

Human Kinetics

Library of Congress Cataloging-in Publication Data

Lee, Mike 1955-
    Moving to discover the USA / Mike Lee, Rhonda L. Clements.
      p.   cm.
    ISBN 0-88011-799-0
    1. Physical education for children--Study and teaching--Activity programs--United States. 2. Movement education--Study and teaching--Activity programs--United States. 3.United States--Study and teaching-Activity programs. I. Clements, Rhonda L.   II. Title.
    GV443.L417 1999
    372.86'044--dc21

98-11700
CIP

ISBN: 0-88011-799-0

Acquisitions Editor: Scott Wikgren; **Developmental Editor:** Elaine Mustain; **Assistant Editors:** Melissa Feld, Phil Natividad; **Copyeditor:** Bonnie Pettifor; **Proofreader:** Erin Cler; **Graphic Designer:** Karen O'Sullivan; **Graphic Artist:** Karen O'Sullivan; **Cover Designer:** Jack Davis; **Cover Photographer:** Tom Roberts; **Illustrator:** Mike Lee; **Printer:** Versa Press

Printed in the United States of America
10 9 8 7 6 5 4 3 2 1

Human Kinetics
Web site: http://www.humankinetics.com/

United States: Human Kinetics, P.O. Box 5076
Champaign, IL 61825-5076
1-800-747-4457
e-mail: humank@hkusa.com

Canada: Human Kinetics, 475 Devonshire Road Unit 100
Windsor, ON N8Y 2L5
1-800-465-7301 (in Canada only)
e-mail: humank@hkcanada.com

Europe: Human Kinetics, P.O. Box IW14
Leeds LS16 6TR, United Kingdom
(44) 1132 781708
e-mail: humank@hkeurope.com

Australia: Human Kinetics, 57A Price Avenue
Lower Mitcham, South Australia 5062
(088) 277 1555
e-mail: humank@hkaustralia.com

New Zealand: Human Kinetics, P.O. Box 105-231
Auckland 1
(09) 523 3462
e-mail: humank@hknewz.com

C O N T E N T S

SECTION THREE: FAMOUS AMERICANS

SECTION FOUR: NATIVE AMERICANS

SECTION FIVE: MAN-MADE LANDMARKS

SECTION SIX: NATURAL WONDERS

SECTION SEVEN: BUILDING A COUNTRY

SECTION EIGHT: TRANSPORTATION

A C K N O W L E D G M E N T S

The authors would like to extend their sincere appreciation to the following teachers, school administrators, and college and university professionals whose expertise greatly strengthened this resource:

Rick Aragona, *Sagamore Children's Center, Dix Hills, NY*
Margot Brous, *The Progressive School of Long Island, NY*
Sammy Chee, Jr., *Monument Valley Elementary School, UT*
Alexandra Gargaglione, *Hofstra University, Hempstead, NY*
Christina Geithner, *Gonzaga University, Spokane, WA*
Eugene Harvey, *Lukachukai Elementary, AR*
Josephine Laham Hasset, *RJO Early Childhood Center, Kings Park, NY*
Bernadette LeBlanc, *Signal Hill School, Dix Hills, NY*
Donna McStay, *Brentwood Elementary School, Brentwood, NY*
Jennifer Nelson, *Gonzaga University, Spokane, WA*
Freyda Rapp, *The Saint Lukes School, New York, NY*
Daisy Riggs, *Department of Head Start, Tuba City, AR*
Susan Sortino, *Columbia Grammar and Prep School, New York, NY*
Marie Testa, *Saw Mill Road Elementary School, North Bellmore, NY*
Carole Weissman, *East Hampton, NY*
Marge Werito, *Navajo Area Indian Health Service, NM*
Lorna Woodward, *Belfast, ME*
Carmelita Yazzi, *Cameron Elementary School, AR*

In addition, the authors would like to thank Dean and Jeannine Lee and Dr. Sylvia J. Giallombardo for their support throughout the process of developing these materials. Special recognition goes to Karen O'Sullivan who skillfully typeset this document.

INTRODUCTION

We have designed *Moving to Discover the USA* to spark the imaginations of children in kindergarten through grade four and to increase their understanding and appreciation of the United States of America. It is also designed to increase the child's ability to move effectively while participating in dynamic learning experiences that reflect the people, symbols, and events associated with the history, geography, geology, and culture of the United States.

We have organized this resource into eight distinctive sections. Each section contains original action rhymes, songs, and games to complement existing elementary school curricula.

Section 1, "Americana," focuses on eight well-known objects and events that reflect our national identity. The concept of democracy is explored through the child's participation in four vigorous games. Symbols that characterize the United States are also explored through physical activity.

Section 2, "This Land," examines the European discovery of America and the establishment and expansion of the states. This theme lends itself to exciting geography lessons, such as when the children take part in a detailed action rhyme to better identify the location of the USA in relationship to other countries.

Section 3, "Famous Americans," introduces children to seven extraordinary individuals who played major roles in securing this country's freedom and shaping its beliefs. Children are encouraged to act out patriotic events and to perform a variety of energetic actions associated with these individuals. In addition, three folklore personalities are included, emphasizing the importance of legendary figures in our national heritage.

Section 4, "Native Americans" acquaints children with the traditional games, homes, dances, and crafts of America's first people. The children's appreciation of these native cultures is enhanced as they participate in creative group activities and in spirited games with authentic rules.

Section 5, "Man-Made Landmarks" directs attention to landmarks typifying major engineering accomplishments. The children will learn about our nation by creating collective body sculptures of five memorials and buildings in our capital city as well as other famous landmarks located throughout the USA.

Section 6, "Natural Wonders," challenges the children to imitate animals and objects common to the Great Lakes, Colorado's Grand Canyon, Wyoming's "Old Faithful Geyser," and the Florida Everglades. It also asks the children to reenact many of the tasks done by the early settlers who lived on the Great Plains of the Midwest.

Section 7, "Building a Country," fosters the child's awareness of factors and groups of people who were instrumental in building a strong country. This section piques interest in the country's early forms of communication, frontier jobs, and vocations. The child's ability to communicate through movement and to demonstrate many tasks associated with America's early cowpokes, miners, lumberjacks, and farmers is emphasized.

Section 8, "Transportation," concludes our examination of the USA by highlighting several forms of transportation that have profoundly affected the expansion of our country. Seventeen activities challenge the child to move in a multitude of ways.

USING *MOVING TO DISCOVER THE USA*

In creating this resource, we have been careful to present materials so they are easy for the teacher to use in the classroom or gymnasium. We have divided each section into smaller subsections. Each subsection has a "theme page" to help the classroom teacher find topics to supplement existing curricula and to provide information for the physical educator who is searching for a series of purposeful physical activities for a daily lesson. All theme pages contain an introductory rhyme, which may be used as a riddle by having children guess the words at the end of each rhyme. The theme page may also include a map or action rhyme to boost the child's desire to participate actively.

You may wish to follow these themes as we have organized them, or you may select topics according to what your students are studying at a particular time. For example, the series of Thanksgiving activities can be used in November, or when the students are studying Early America in the classroom; visit the various man-made and natural wonders as students discuss the states in social studies; meet Harriet Tubman during Black History month (February); and ride a tornado with Pecos Bill after the children have read about him in language arts. Regardless of when you decide to use these materials, the addition of movement will make your cross-curricular teaching more exciting.

We have also designed the activities so that teachers having limited or no equipment will not be restricted in their use of this book, although we do recommend the use of flags or colored jerseys to identify groups of children when participating in tagging games. We also suggest that the teacher identify the "chaser" or child tagging his or her peers by having the individual wear an armband, or carry a ball or some other distinguishing item that can be clearly seen by all fleeing participants. Similarly, it may be helpful to have all children practice the basic movement skill before attempting to organize the game, song, or dance activity. This suggestion increases the likelihood that all children will experience success. In all situations, teachers should attend to the child's safety and provide ample space for a risk-free learning environment. Now it's time to begin *Moving to Discover the USA!*

The following information briefly describes the key components of the text.

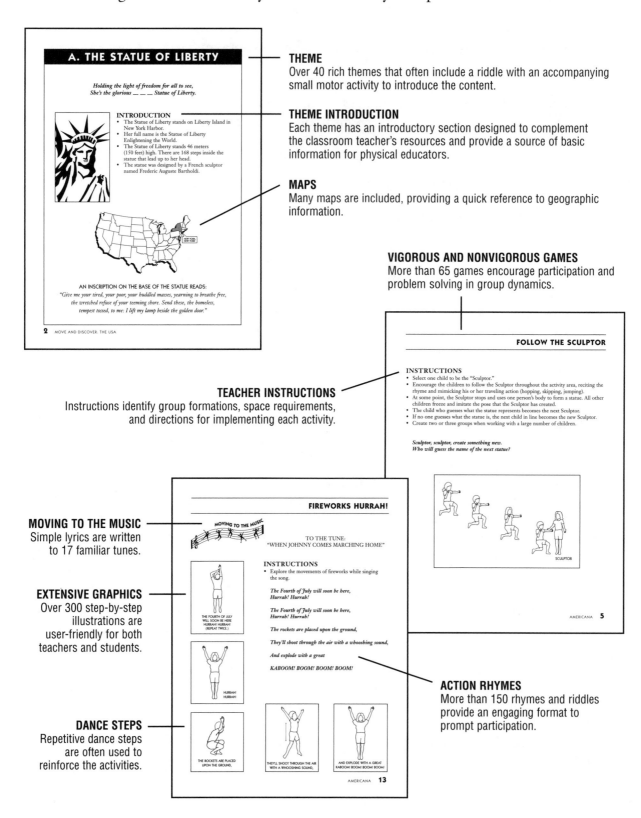

THEME
Over 40 rich themes that often include a riddle with an accompanying small motor activity to introduce the content.

THEME INTRODUCTION
Each theme has an introductory section designed to complement the classroom teacher's resources and provide a source of basic information for physical educators.

MAPS
Many maps are included, providing a quick reference to geographic information.

VIGOROUS AND NONVIGOROUS GAMES
More than 65 games encourage participation and problem solving in group dynamics.

TEACHER INSTRUCTIONS
Instructions identify group formations, space requirements, and directions for implementing each activity.

MOVING TO THE MUSIC
Simple lyrics are written to 17 familiar tunes.

EXTENSIVE GRAPHICS
Over 300 step-by-step illustrations are user-friendly for both teachers and students.

DANCE STEPS
Repetitive dance steps are often used to reinforce the activities.

ACTION RHYMES
More than 150 rhymes and riddles provide an engaging format to prompt participation.

AMERICANA

Americana, symbols of this country,
Remind us to be thankful for democracy.

A. THE STATUE OF LIBERTY

Holding the light of freedom for all to see,
She's the glorious __ __ __ Statue of Liberty.

INTRODUCTION
*   The Statue of Liberty stands on Liberty Island in New York Harbor.
*   Her full name is the Statue of Liberty Enlightening the World.
*   The Statue of Liberty stands 46 meters (150 feet) high. There are 168 steps inside the statue that lead up to her head.
*   The statue was designed by a French sculptor named Frederic Auguste Bartholdi.

NEW YORK, NEW YORK

AN INSCRIPTION ON THE BASE OF THE STATUE READS:
"Give me your tired, your poor, your huddled masses, yearning to breathe free, the wretched refuse of your teeming shore. Send these, the homeless, tempest tossed, to me: I lift my lamp beside the golden door."

Liberty's torch beckons everyone to shore,
Welcoming the homeless, the tired, and the poor.

INSTRUCTIONS
- Read the verse slowly as the children imitate the actions through movement.
- Create paper crowns and torches.

Let's pretend we are
  The Statue of Liberty
Welcoming everyone
  To the land of the free.

How does the proud
  Statue of Liberty stand?
Reach and stretch, holding the
  Torch of Liberty
    In your right hand.

How would she stand ...
If she held the torch
  In her left hand?

Now make Liberty grow,
Stretch even higher, and stand tiptoe.

IMAGINARY STATUES

INSTRUCTIONS

- Organize the children in a large circle.
- Challenge the children to act out the movements in the action rhyme.

  A statue can represent anything,
  An important invention or a bird on the wing.

  How would a statue of your parents look?
  Make believe you are a statue of a teacher ...
  A doctor ... a fire fighter ... or a cook.

  If you were a statue what would you be?
  An eagle, a horse, or perhaps a tree?

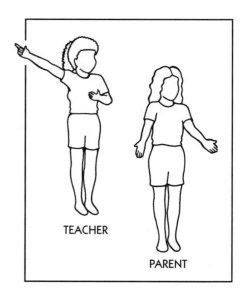

TEACHER

PARENT

- Encourage partners to combine their bodies and create a statue to demonstrate the following feelings and attitudes: fearless, heroic, proud, mighty, bold, curious, adventurous, daring.

SILLY STATUES

INSTRUCTIONS

- Encourage the children to move throughout the activity area assuming silly poses (bashful, droopy, floppy, clumsy, wicked, playful, and grumpy).
- On the signal, "Silly statue, stop!" all children freeze in their current position.

Silly statues stretch and bend,
Twist and turn from end to end.

FOLLOW THE SCULPTOR

INSTRUCTIONS
- Select one child to be the "Sculptor."
- Encourage the children to follow the Sculptor throughout the activity area, reciting the rhyme and mimicking his or her traveling action (hopping, skipping, jumping).
- At some point, the Sculptor stops and uses one person's body to form a statue. All other children freeze and imitate the pose that the Sculptor has created.
- The child who guesses what the statue represents becomes the next Sculptor.
- If no one guesses what the statue is, the next child in line becomes the new Sculptor.
- Create two or three groups when working with a large number of children.

Sculptor, sculptor, create something new.
Who will guess the name of the next statue?

SCULPTOR

LIBERTY SAYS

People immigrate from the North, South, East, and West.
To become a citizen they must take a test.

INSTRUCTIONS

- Organize the children into four equal groups in each corner of the activity area. Name the groups: North, South, East, West.
- Designate one child to represent the "Statue of Liberty," who stands in the center of the activity area at an equal distance from each group.
- The individuals in the groups hold hands unless the movement requires the hands to be free.
- Play is similar to "Simon Says." When Liberty raises one arm and gives the command, "Liberty says" all the children perform the movement command until Liberty says, "Statue, stop!"

EXAMPLE: "LIBERTY SAYS ..."

Hop on one foot	Hop to the side	Balance on one foot
Turn in a circle	Form a circle	March in place
Run in place	Leap forward	Gallop to the right
Walk forward	Twist an upper body part	Jump up and down
Reach for the sky	Crab walk forward	Tiptoe forward
Take giant steps	Skip forward	Clap your hands
Stamp your feet	Dance and move your hips	Kneel on one knee
Crawl forward	Step backward	Swing your arms
Roll over	Sink to a low level	Bob up and down

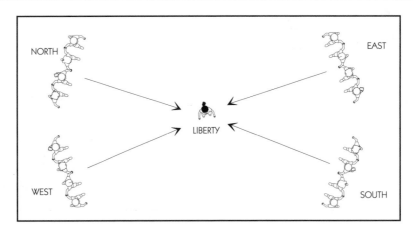

- Liberty alternates the commands by saying: "Statue says ... now ... or OK...."
- The children may only move when the command is, "Liberty says...."
- If a member moves at the wrong command, his or her group misses one turn.
- The game continues until one group reaches the Statue of Liberty and all group members become citizens.

B. THE STARS AND STRIPES

A blue sky with 50 stars,
Surrounded by red and white bars.

Old Glory flying free,
Symbol of our liberty.

The Stars and Stripes, may they always wave
Above the land of the free and home of the __ brave.

INTRODUCTION
- The Stars and Stripes symbolizes the land, people, and beliefs of the USA.
- The American flag has three names: The Stars and Stripes, Old Glory, and the Star-Spangled Banner.
- The "Pledge of Allegiance" was first printed in a magazine for children.
- Each of the colors on the flag has a meaning: red–strength, white–virtue, blue–justice.

THE FIRST OFFICIAL FLAG OF THE UNITED STATES

FLAG FLYING

INSTRUCTIONS

- Ask the children to select partners and respond to the action rhyme as you read it aloud.
- Create paper flags in class.
- Recite the "Pledge of Allegiance."

It's time to raise the flag into the sky.
One partner pulls the rope, the other
  Is the flag, rising from low to high.

Reach and pull hand over hand,
Raising the Stars and Stripes over the land.

If the flag doesn't have a light,
It must come down at night.

Slowly lower your
  Body to bring
    The flag down.
Be careful,
  It must not
    Touch the ground.

- Exchange roles.

BETSY ROSS MADE A FLAG

TO THE TUNE:
"THE MULBERRY BUSH"

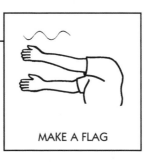

This is how Betsy Ross made the flag,
Made the flag, made the flag.
This is the way she made the flag,
To fly high in the sky.
- Wave your arms like a flag.

First rip seven red stripes of cloth,
Red stripes of cloth, red stripes of cloth.
First rip seven red stripes of cloth,
To sew into the flag.
- Grasp an imaginary piece of cloth. Quickly fling your arms outward and pretend to tear seven long pieces of cloth.

Then rip six white stripes of cloth,
White stripes of cloth, white stripes of cloth.
Then rip six white stripes of cloth,
To sew into the flag.
- Grasp an imaginary sheet of cloth and tear it six times to create white stripes.

Stretch out wide to make a star,
To make a star, to make a star.
Stretch out wide to make a star,
For each state in the union.
- Stretch your arms and legs outward to create a five-pointed star.

Thread your needle and start to sew,
Start to sew, start to sew.
Thread your needle and start to sew,
Until your flag is finished.
- Grasp the imaginary cloth in one hand and sew by pulling the long thread high above your head.

This is the way Washington flew the flag,
Flew the flag, flew the flag.
This is the way he flew the flag,
High in the sky.
- Wave one hand like a flag rising up a flag pole.

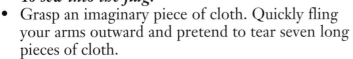

MAKE A FLAG

RIP THE CLOTH
(13 TIMES)

MAKE 13 STARS

THREAD NEEDLE & SEW

FLY THE FLAG

RIBBON FLAGS

INSTRUCTIONS
- Cut red, white, and blue ribbons or cloth into three-foot strips.
- Provide each child with one or two strips.
- Upon completion, play the "Stars and Stripes Forever" by John Philip Sousa, challenging the children to create their own marching patterns.

1. *Raise your flag from the earth to the sky.*
   Wave it down low ...
     In the middle ... then up high.

2. *How would your flag flow*
   If the wind was blowing slow?
   What if a strong wind began to blow?

3. *What would your flag do*
   If the wind blew from someplace new?

4. *Can you wave your flag to the left and right? Now up and down ...*
   Then like the hands of a clock, wave them around and around.

5. *Who can wave their ribbons to create different shapes in the air?*
   Try a circle ... a triangle ... a spiral ... and a square.

6. *Match a partner's movements like an image in a mirror.*
   Matching mirror movements magically appear.

7. *See if you can spell names and words in the air.*
   Now write a secret message for a partner to share.

8. *Let's join partners together in a group and form a four-line marching troop.*
   Imagine the four of you are marching in a parade with your flags proudly displayed.

9. *All the wind can do is blow.*
   Work with four new friends and put on a show.

10. *The wind makes flags fly.*
    You can, too, if you try!

C. INDEPENDENCE DAY

On the first Independence Day the Liberty Bell rang.
Today, the __ __ __ Fourth of July, ends with a bang.

INTRODUCTION
* In 1776 the United States declared independence from England.
* Each July 4th, Americans celebrate the Declaration of Independence with fireworks.
* Fireworks are rockets that explode when burned, producing brilliant lighting effects.
* The Chinese invented fireworks in the sixth century.

WHOOSH! The rockets fly,

KABOOM! Exploding in the sky.

With a flash, the explosion booms, and SPARKLES down in colorful plumes.

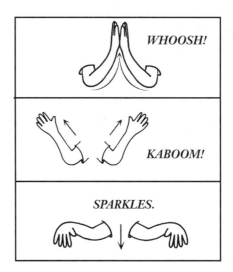

WHOOSH!

KABOOM!

SPARKLES.

SAFETY FIRST!!!
* Only adults should light real fireworks.
* Never play with fireworks!
* Fireworks are illegal in many states.

ROCKETS AWAY

INSTRUCTIONS
- Tell the children to scatter throughout the activity area and imitate the movements in the action rhyme.

Make-believe you are
  A rocket; crouch down low.
Imagine you are ready to blow.

Light your fuses,
  Make a hissing sound.
HISSSS! Get ready
  To blast off from the ground.

Rockets blast off!
  WHOOSH! You flare,
Rising high up in the air.

KABOOM!
  Exploding with light,
Brilliant colors
  Fill the night.

Expanding into a fiery crown,
Twinkling sparks
  Shower down.

Soon another rocket
  Is ready to fire.
Will this one soar even higher?

YOU LIGHT UP THE SKY

INSTRUCTIONS
- Have the children form lines of four to six children each and crouch down to a low level.
- The first child in each line lights each make-believe rocket.
- When the lighters reach the end of the line, they become rockets.
- The players lower their bodies once again, and the new children at the front of the lines pretend to light the fuses.

All the rockets are in a line.
Each will fill the sky with a fiery design.

People light the rockets,
One after the other.

They shoot into the sky,
First one, then another.

HISSSS! WHOOSH! KABOOM!

MOVING TO THE MUSIC

TO THE TUNE:
"WHEN JOHNNY COMES MARCHING HOME"

INSTRUCTIONS

- Explore the movements of fireworks while singing the song.

The Fourth of July will soon be here,
Hurrah! Hurrah!

The Fourth of July will soon be here,
Hurrah! Hurrah!

The rockets are placed upon the ground,

They'll shoot through the air with a whooshing sound,

And explode with a great

KABOOM! BOOM! BOOM! BOOM!

THE FOURTH OF JULY
WILL SOON BE HERE
HURRAH! HURRAH!
(REPEAT TWICE.)

HURRAH!
HURRAH!

THE ROCKETS ARE PLACED
UPON THE GROUND,

THEY'LL SHOOT THROUGH THE AIR
WITH A WHOOSHING SOUND,

AND EXPLODE WITH A GREAT
KABOOM! BOOM! BOOM! BOOM!

FIREWORKS PATTERNS

Fireworks explode in many different ways,
Creating colorful and noisy displays.

INSTRUCTIONS

- Explain to the children that fireworks are designed to explode and create many different patterns. Each pattern has a special name such as willow, palm tree, or chrysanthemum.
- The people who create fireworks are called *pyrotechnists*, which means "fire artists."
- Organize the children into groups of three, four, or five.
- Challenge the groups to invent fireworks movement patterns with everyone in each group moving together.
- They may shoot upward, blow to one side, "rain" down, form a circle, twirl and spin, or create more than one explosion.
- Have them draw stick figures to illustrate their activities.
- Encourage each group to demonstrate and teach their pattern to the class.
- Whenever possible, play patriotic music during a class performance of the completed patterns.

COUNT DOWN
FROM 10

SHOOT UPWARD

RAIN DOWN

D. THANKSGIVING

The Pilgrims had a hard time living,
But thanks to the American Indians,
We have __ Thanksgiving.

INTRODUCTION

- Thanksgiving is celebrated on the fourth Thursday of November.
- The holiday is attributed to a thanksgiving festival held by the Plymouth colony in 1621.
- Turkey was served on the first Thanksgiving by the Pilgrims.
- In America, native fruits and vegetables, turkeys, and pumpkin pie have become traditional foods for the day.

ASK THE CHILDREN TO MAKE A LIST OF ALL THE REASONS THEY HAVE TO BE THANKFUL.

THANKSGIVING SHARING

The Pilgrims needed help to survive.
Friendly American Indians kept them alive.

INSTRUCTIONS

- Copy a set of the Thanksgiving exchange cards (see page 17) for each student.
- Have the children form two equal lines on opposite ends of the activity area.
- One group represents the "Pilgrims" and the other group represents "American Indians."
- The Pilgrims call out the first line from the first card, followed by the response line from the American Indians.
- The two lines meet each other in the center of the activity area and exchange cards and roles.
- Both groups return to their original positions and switch roles. The new Pilgrims call out the first line from the second card, followed by the response line from the new American Indians.
- Play continues through card number 5.
- Both groups form a circle while reading the last verse.

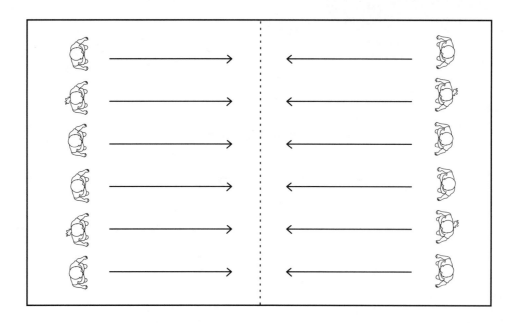

THANKSGIVING EXCHANGE CARDS

1	**MEAT**	

Pilgrims:
"Please, we need something to eat!"
American Indians:
"We'll jump halfway over with some meat."

4	**SQUASH**	

Pilgrims:
"May we have some squash for our stew?"
American Indians:
"Hop on one foot and please say, 'thank you'."

2	**SEEDS**	

Pilgrims:
"We would like a garden, may we have some seeds?"
American Indians:
"We'll skip on over to fill your needs."

5	**CORN**	

Pilgrims:
"Please, may we have some corn to make our bread?"
American Indians:
"Walk towards us backward, but turn your head."

3	**TURKEY**	

Pilgrims:
"We would like a turkey for Thanksgiving Day!"
American Indians:
"We'll run one over, meet us halfway."

6	**DINNER**	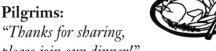

Pilgrims:
"Thanks for sharing, please join our dinner!"
American Indians:
"By helping each other, everyone is a winner!"

THANKSGIVING DAY FEAST

INSTRUCTIONS

- Challenge the children to identify several fruits, meats, vegetables, and other foods that are common to a Thanksgiving Day feast. Have each child select one food to be identified with before the activity begins.
- Select one "Pilgrim" and one "American Indian" who clasp hands and stand in the middle of the playing area. All other players stand side by side on the four sides of the activity area.
- On the teacher's signal, the Pilgrim and the American Indian decide upon one food product and announce that item to the group. Only the player(s) representing that food product dash to the opposite side of the playing area in an effort to avoid being tagged by the Pilgrim and American Indian.
- Any fruits, meats, or vegetables that are tagged clasp hands with the American Indian and Pilgrim and work together to repeat the action.
- Vary the form of traveling action used to move to the opposite side of the activity area.
- Encourage students from different ethnic groups to identify special foods served during the holiday.

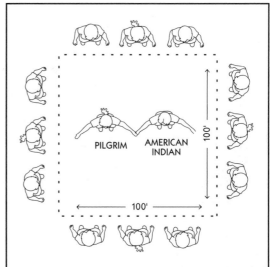

SAMPLE FOOD PRODUCTS

Onions	Ham	Yams
Corn	Beef	Grapes
Squash	Cranberries	Lettuce
Peas	Pumpkin	Cauliflower
Carrots	Potatoes	Pears
Turkey	Tomatoes	Baked apples
Roast duck	Bread	Cornbread
Plum pudding	Mince pie	Biscuits

Fast runners, who can also fly,
"Gobble, gobble" is their cry.

INSTRUCTIONS

- Generate enthusiasm by telling the children that Benjamin Franklin wanted the turkey to be the national bird of the USA. Male turkeys are called "toms" or "gobblers," and females are called "hens." Young turkeys are called "poults."
- Explain that wild turkeys eat nuts, roots, seeds, and leaf buds and roost high in trees. When the Pilgrims and Indians hunted the wild fowl, they followed the turkey's foot tracks in the mud or snow, and listened for its loud "gobble, gobble, gobble."
- To begin, print the word "TURKEY" in one-inch capital letters on a sheet of paper. Since the word "turkey" contains six letters, the word needs to be printed five times for a group of 30 children, or six times for a group of 36 children, and so on to ensure that each child has a letter.
- On the teacher's signal, all children begin strutting throughout the activity area searching for other children to spell the word T-U-R-K-E-Y.
- As each child locates a player holding a letter he or she is seeking, the two players link arms and continue the strutting movement while seeking additional children.
- No child may link arms with players other than those having the letter immediately preceding or following his or her letter.
- As each six-member group is formed, the players continue to strut and make gobbling sounds, until all children are linked.
- Create a wild card with the letter "S" when working with an odd number of children.

Gobble, gobble!

E. THE LIBERTY BELL

It rang for the Declaration of Independence.
Freedom is what it represents.

When the American people became free,
It rang for their liberty.

It has a crack now, can you tell?
I'm talking about the __ __ Liberty Bell.

INTRODUCTION

- The word *liberty* means "freedom, or the release from being controlled."
- The Liberty Bell was originally made in England and was transported to Philadelphia where it rang loudly on the first Independence Day in 1776 and every year until 1835 when it cracked.
- It weighs over 945 kilograms (2,080 pounds).
- The Liberty Bell is still on display in Philadelphia, Pennsylvania.

PHILADELPHIA, PENNSYLVANIA

AN INSCRIPTION ON THE BELL READS:

"Proclaim Liberty Throughout All The Land Unto All The Inhabitants Thereof."

THE OLD LIBERTY BELL

TO THE TUNE:
"THE OLD GREY MARE"

INSTRUCTIONS

• Alternate between the movements while singing each verse of the song.

*The Old Liberty Bell doesn't
Ring like it used to ring,
Ring like it used to ring,
Ring like it used to ring.*

*The Old Liberty Bell doesn't
Ring like it used to ring,
Way back in 1776.*

TAKE THREE STEPS FORWARD
AS YOU MOVE UP AND DOWN.

*The Old Liberty Bell is
Cracked so they don't let it swing,
Cracked so they don't let it swing,
Cracked so they don't let it swing.*

*The Old Liberty Bell doesn't
Ring like it used to ring,
Way back in 1776.*

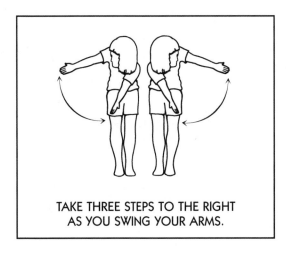

TAKE THREE STEPS TO THE RIGHT
AS YOU SWING YOUR ARMS.

BUDDY BELL

INSTRUCTIONS

- Organize the children into groups of five.
- Four children grasp hands to form a circle. One child is the gong and stands in the center of the circle.
- The circle players move back and forth three or four steps like the movement of a bell swinging.
- The center player also begins to move from side to side.
- Everyone recites the verse and makes a bell sound when the gong touches a side of the bell.

Together our bodies are the Liberty Bell,
Swinging, ringing, wishing the country well.

Back and forth, side to side, Clang! Clang! Clang!
Everyone listened when the Liberty Bell rang.

INSTRUCTIONS

- Talk about how bells were used to announce special occasions or to bring people together.
- In early America, a town crier walked along the city streets ringing a bell and shouting the latest news.
- Provide each child with a slip of paper and a pencil.
- Each child creates an action word or phrase that describes a movement and prints it on the piece of paper. Older children may create complete sentences, short instructional rhymes, or stories with multiple movements.
- Offer the following action words to stimulate creativity: run, jump, touch, stand, hop, spin, walk, shake, gallop, skip, crawl, creep, wobble, wiggle, prance, stomp, stamp, tiptoe, fly, scamper, spring, scurry, strut, march, charge, reach, twist, duck, lift, clap, hold, shiver, push, turn, rise, fall.
- Organize the children into a large circle and place a bell in the center of the circle.
- Each child takes a turn running to the center of the circle and becoming the town crier by ringing the bell and saying, "Hear ye! Hear ye!"
- The town crier then reads and performs his or her action phrase as the other children imitate the movements.

Hear ye! Hear ye!
Hop, jump, and run in place,
Keep a smile on your face.

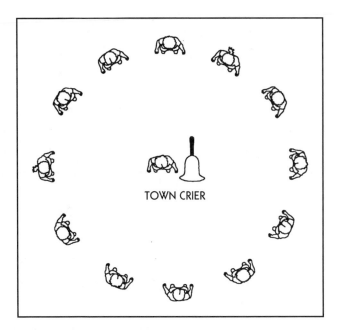

TOWN CRIER

Peace and strength are on display
Through this symbol of the USA.

Our national bird appears very regal.
An olive branch and arrows are held by the __ __ bald eagle.

INTRODUCTION

- Eagles are birds of prey belonging to the raptor family.
- The bald eagle was adopted as the national bird of the USA in 1782.
- Benjamin Franklin wanted the turkey to be our national symbol.
- Birds of prey are known for their hooked beaks, keen vision, and large talons.

INSTRUCTIONS

- Inform the children that the Great Seal is the official stamp of the USA. It means "This is the property of the United States of America."
- The eagle holds a banner that reads, *"E Pluribus Unum,"* which in Latin means "Out of many, one."
- Encourage the children to use their bodies to create the pose of the eagle displayed on the Great Seal of the USA.
- After posing, have the children work together to create a classroom seal.

Imagine you are proud and regal,
The symbol of the USA, the bald eagle.

Hold your arms wide
And slowly turn your head to the side.

Open your legs; one claw holds the olive branch.
That means you first give peace a chance.

The other holds arrows to show you are strong,
That you will stand for right against wrong.

THE SOARING EAGLE

Once bald eagles soared across all of the USA.
There were many more than we have today.

INSTRUCTIONS
- Remind the children that bald eagles often live near lakes, rivers, or the ocean where they can catch fish to eat. They soar high above the water searching for fish with their keen eyes.
- When an eagle spies a fish, it twists its body to the side and swoops down, grasping the fish with its claws.
- Have each child cut out 10 paper fish and number them from 5 to 15.
- Scatter the paper fish, numbers down, throughout the activity area.
- The numbers represent the number of wing flaps and steps the children can take after picking up a fish.
- On the teacher's signal "Fly eagles!" each child runs, flapping his or her arms, to the nearest fish and swoops down to pick it up.
- Each child then flaps arms and steps forward according to the number written on the fish selected.
- The child must swoop to snatch a new fish after completing the number of steps found on the fish.
- Remind the children that eagles never fly into the pathway of another eagle.
- The children continue to "fly" throughout the activity area until all fish are collected.

Fresh fish is your favorite treat,
Swoop and dive to catch one to eat.

Fly until your number runs low,
Then catch another in the water below.

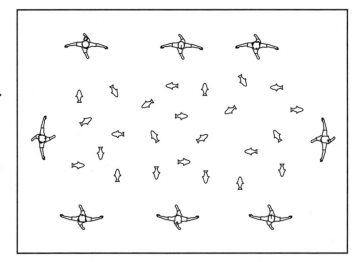

G. DEMOCRACY

We the people have our way,
Voting is how we have our say.

The people choose the leaders and remain free.
That is why the USA is a __ democracy.

INTRODUCTION
- Democracy is the form of government practiced in the USA.
- The people of the USA elect leaders who create and enforce laws.
- There are local officials such as mayors and city councils who govern cities, state leaders, and federal officials who create laws for the entire country.
- The most important laws are the Constitution and the Bill of Rights.

DEMOCRACY IN ACTION

INSTRUCTIONS
- Organize the children into a large circle around the activity area.
- Read the following example and have the children demonstrate the action.

EXAMPLE
The City Councillor says, "Hop!"
The Mayor says, "Stop."
The Governor says, "Rub your stomach and pat your head."
The Representative says, "Spin in circles instead."
The Senator says, "Reach for the skies."
The President says, "Blink your eyes."
The People say, "That's not what we want to do! So we'll vote for someone new."

- Select six children to move to the center of the circle and give each the name of an elected official written on both sides of a large sheet of paper.
- Challenge each official to create an action word or phrase. The teacher then follows the sequence of officials in the example.
- The children in the circle represent the people and perform each new action. Together they recite the final line and the teacher selects six new officials from the circle.
- Continue the activity until everyone has had an opportunity to be an elected official.
- End the game by having all children join hands and recite the following verse:

We the people live free,
Thanks to our democracy.

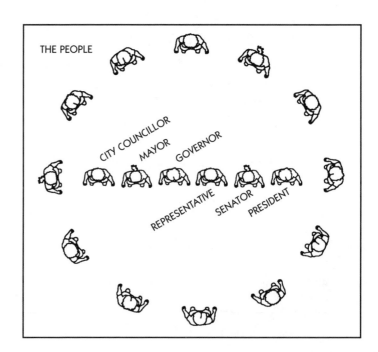

THE BALANCE OF POWER

To create a new law, everyone must agree.
The balance of power helps keep us all free.

INSTRUCTIONS

- Reinforce the idea that in order to create a new law the Senate or the House of Representatives must write a bill. The President must sign the bill before it becomes a law.
- Divide the children into two equal groups. One group is the Senate; the other is the House of Representatives.
- Place a hoop or other marker on the floor to represent the Capitol building.
- Select one child to be the President. To begin the activity, the President calls,

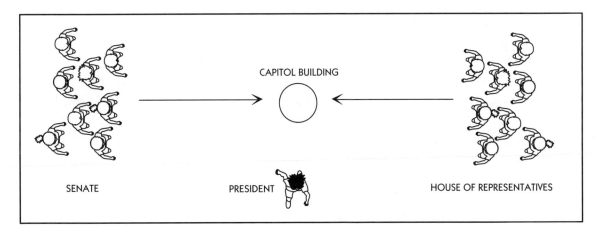

SENATE   CAPITOL BUILDING   PRESIDENT   HOUSE OF REPRESENTATIVES

Senate be nimble, House be quick,
Creating a law is the trick!

- This action signals the two groups to merge, and individuals from opposite groups find partners and grasp hands to create "Bills." The newly developed Bills call out:

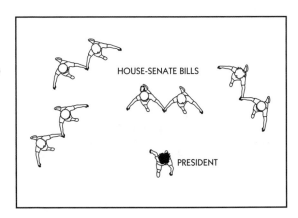

HOUSE-SENATE BILLS   PRESIDENT

Making a new law is our plan
We'll catch you if we can.

- The first set of Bills to tag the President on the shoulder and run back to the Capitol becomes a Law.
- Vary the type of traveling action used to tag the President (e.g., galloping, skipping, hopping).

UNITING THE STATES

INSTRUCTIONS

- State that the USA is a country with laws that unite the states.
- Each year, new laws are created by the Representatives and Senators; these must be signed by the President to become law. When there is a problem in the country a new law is written.
- Have each child create a hand-sized circle of paper and print the words "A LAW" on it.
- Place all the law circles in a hoop or box (that represents Washington, D.C.) in the center of a large activity area.
- Select three children to become "Lawmakers" (the President, a Representative, and a Senator). They stand near "Washington, D.C."
- The remaining children represent the "States" and form a large circle around Washington, D.C.
- The game begins when the teacher says, "Run away, run away, States."
- A Lawmaker must then tag a State and pass the law circle on to that player.
- Any State that is tagged may tag another State and pass the law circle on to that player. No one may tag a State that is already carrying a law circle.
- After a law circle is given away, the Lawmaker or State returns to Washington, D.C., picks up a new law circle, and tries to tag another State.
- When all the States are carrying a law circle, the groups unite by joining hands around Washington, D.C. and recite the following verse:

The laws of our country unite our lands,
Like a circle of friends holding hands.

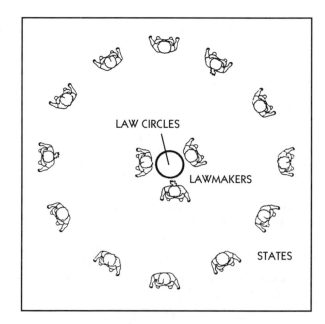

INSTRUCTIONS

- Select three children to be "Lawmakers" (the President, a Representative, and a Senator).
- Secure a puzzle of the United States, and distribute the pieces to the remaining children who represent the "States."
- On the teacher's signal, all States flee from the Lawmakers.
- As a State is tagged by a Lawmaker, he or she gathers to the side of the activity area and assists the other tagged States in assembling the puzzle.
- When working with small groups, give players two to three state pieces each. In this situation, a tagged State may reenter the game after correctly placing one puzzle piece. He or she continues to flee until being tagged again and so on until all pieces are correctly placed and the puzzle is completed.

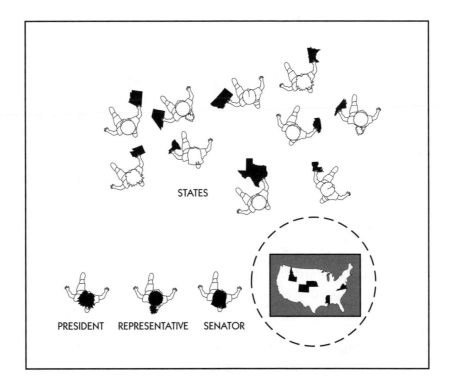

STATES

PRESIDENT   REPRESENTATIVE   SENATOR

People have come to the USA from everywhere.
They have all brought different things to share.

Customs, clothing, and food can be found
From the wide world all around.

The USA and the world share a lot
That's why USA is called the __ __ melting pot.

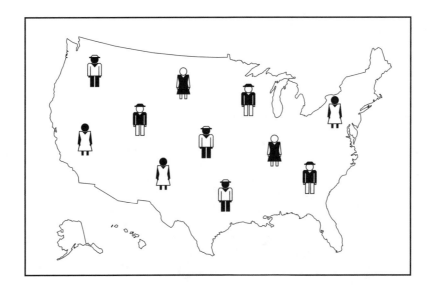

INTRODUCTION
- The first immigrants to this country crossed a land bridge from Asia over 30,000 years ago. The early colonists arrived by ship from Europe.
- African people were forced to come to this country as slaves.
- Many Asian people sailed to the West Coast where they helped build the growing country.
- People came for religious freedom, to escape poverty, or just for adventure. New people still come to this country for many of the same reasons.

A GLOBAL FEAST

Foreign food is great to eat,
It makes dinner an international treat.

INSTRUCTIONS
• Challenge the children to use their bodies to explore the shapes of international foods.

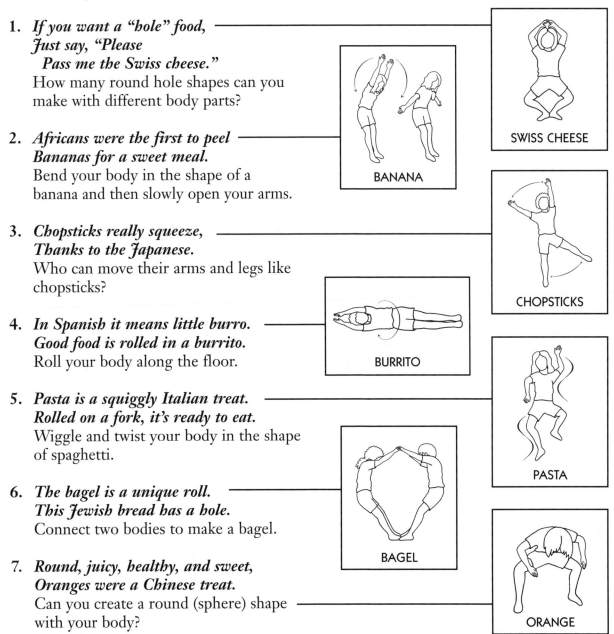

1. *If you want a "hole" food,*
   Just say, "Please
   Pass me the Swiss cheese."
   How many round hole shapes can you
   make with different body parts?

2. *Africans were the first to peel*
   Bananas for a sweet meal.
   Bend your body in the shape of a
   banana and then slowly open your arms.

3. *Chopsticks really squeeze,*
   Thanks to the Japanese.
   Who can move their arms and legs like
   chopsticks?

4. *In Spanish it means little burro.*
   Good food is rolled in a burrito.
   Roll your body along the floor.

5. *Pasta is a squiggly Italian treat.*
   Rolled on a fork, it's ready to eat.
   Wiggle and twist your body in the shape
   of spaghetti.

6. *The bagel is a unique roll.*
   This Jewish bread has a hole.
   Connect two bodies to make a bagel.

7. *Round, juicy, healthy, and sweet,*
   Oranges were a Chinese treat.
   Can you create a round (sphere) shape
   with your body?

SWISS CHEESE

BANANA

CHOPSTICKS

BURRITO

PASTA

BAGEL

ORANGE

THE CHINESE NEW YEAR DRAGON DANCE

There is no reason to be afraid,
This dragon is leading the Chinese New Year parade.

INSTRUCTIONS

- Relate how the Chinese New Year is celebrated in many cities in the USA. It lasts four days and is called Hsin Nien, in Chinese. The Chinese calendar has 12 months, and the Chinese New Year occurs in the month of January or February.
- Reveal that the highlight of the Chinese New Year parade is a long dragon puppet that is controlled by a line of people who dance inside its body.
- Divide the children into two or three groups.
- Ask the members of each group to place their hands on the shoulders or waist of the person in front of them and stomp, slither, scuff, march, trudge, or strut to create a group dragon dance.
- For a more elaborate dragon, supply the children with markers to paint a large balloon to resemble a dragon's head or use the balloon as a mold for a papier-mâché dragon's head.
- Sew or safety-pin old bed sheets together to create a puppet's body and color it with markers and paint.
- Whenever possible, play authentic Chinese music while the children perform their dances.

Place your hands on the person in front of you to make
A long dragon that moves like a snake.

Move up and down and side to side,
Staying together as you stride.

Who can make the sound of dragon's roar,
While moving like a giant dinosaur?

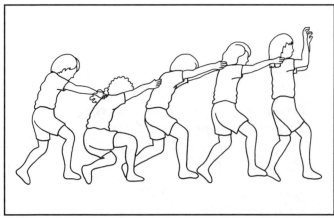

THIS LAND

European colonists came and the land was divided.
They created states and fought for a new country united.

They traveled on foot and across the sea,
Their journeys led them to a new __ country.

INTRODUCTION

- Exploration means traveling to unknown regions for purposes of discovery.
- Native Americans were the first people to explore and live on North America's soil.
- The Viking explorers sailed to North America in small ships with a single sail and long oars. Spanish explorers were seeking an ocean route to Asia.
- Explorers like Daniel Boone and Lewis and Clark expanded our knowledge of the USA's frontier.

EXPLORERS OF THE NEW WORLD

Explorers have always traveled to new places
In search of resources and wide-open spaces.

INSTRUCTIONS
- Encourage the children to demonstrate the movements of the early explorers.

THE FIRST PEOPLE
American Indians came to this land
  Thousands of years ago,
Exactly when, we do not know.
They walked to this country
On a land bridge across the Bering Sea.
- Who can walk like the proud American Indians?

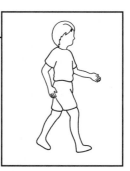

THE VIKINGS
Vikings crossed the North Sea,
The first was Leif Ericsson
  In the 10th century.
They rowed across in a mighty ship
To make the first Atlantic Ocean trip.
- Stretch your arms forward, then pull the heavy oar toward your chest.

COLUMBUS
The wind blew Columbus's
  Sailing ships here in 1492.
He came in search of trade and revenue.
- Raise your arms like the sails on a ship being blown by the wind.

THE CONQUISTADORS
Spanish conquistadors
  Were the first to bring horses
To America's shores.
- Prance like a Spanish pony and clap your hands on your thighs to make the sound of a horse's hooves.

EXPLORERS OF THE NEW WORLD (Continued)

THE WILDERNESS ROAD

Daniel Boone chopped down trees
  To build the Wilderness Road.
Across the Appalachian Mountains
  New settlers flowed.

- Make-believe you are chopping down a tree.

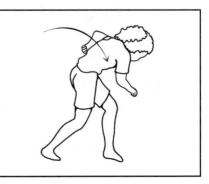

LEWIS AND CLARK

Lewis and Clark traveled
  From St. Louis, Missouri,
To claim the Oregon territory.
They traveled on foot and by canoe.
With the help of Sacajawea,
  The United States grew.

- Imagine you are paddling a canoe down a wild river.

WAGON TRAINS

Settlers traveled West
  In covered wagon trains,
Rocking side to side
  As they crossed the Great Plains.

- Form a covered wagon shape with your arms and rock from side to side.

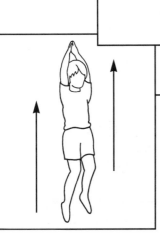

THE LAST FRONTIER

New explorers dream
  Of the moon and Mars
As they blast off flying
  Toward the stars.

- Pretend your body is the space shuttle blasting off into space.

B. THE STATES

As the pioneers traveled to new territories,
They built roads, bridges, farms, and cities.

Working together they would cooperate
To join the USA and form a new ___ state.

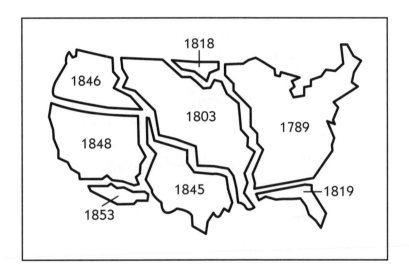

INTRODUCTION
- The first states were created in 1789 to give definite boundaries to large territories of land.
- The first 13 states were on the East Coast.
- Each of our 50 states has a unique shape.
- In terms of land size, Alaska is the largest state and Rhode Island is the smallest.

THE USA TODAY

The states are united in liberty,
So everyone can live safe and free.

INSTRUCTIONS

- Use your hands to count to 50 by 10s.
- Make the motion of waves with your hands.
- Move your arms like grain blowing in the wind.
- Raise your arms to form a mountain peak.

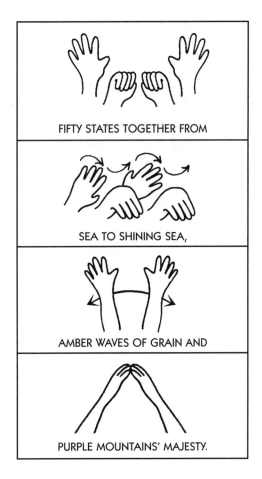

Fifty states together from
Sea to shining sea,
Amber waves of grain and
Purple mountains' majesty.

HAWAIIAN ISLAND HOPSCOTCH

A chain of islands in the sea,
The 50th state is Hawaii.

INSTRUCTIONS
- Identify Hawaii's nickname as being "The Aloha State." Explain that the islands were formed from volcanoes that rose from the bottom of the Pacific Ocean.
- Ask the children to form a side-by-side line along one side of the activity area.
- Hop forward eight times on one foot, jump on two feet, and finish on one foot for the first verse.
- Hop forward one time for each item, stopping to form the shape or movement of each one.

Hop and jump between the eight islands that form a chain.
- Move forward eight times by hopping on one foot, jumping on two feet, hopping on one foot.

Plump pineapples, erupting volcanoes, and swaying sugarcane.
- Form a large round shape, a pointed "mountain" that explodes, a tall swaying movement.

Say "hello" or "good-bye" with an "aloha."
- Extend arms and wave good-bye.

Surf a wave, paddle an outrigger canoe, and do a hula.
- Pretend to surf, paddle, and sway hips and move arms.

PINEAPPLE   VOLCANO   SUGARCANE   HELLO   GOOD-BYE   SURF   PADDLE   HULA

STATE SHAPE STRETCH

Can you move your body into the shape of a state?
How many states can your body create?

INSTRUCTIONS

- Secure pictures of the states identified in the activity. Instruct the children to hold each stretch for at least 10 seconds and to stop stretching if their muscles begin to hurt.

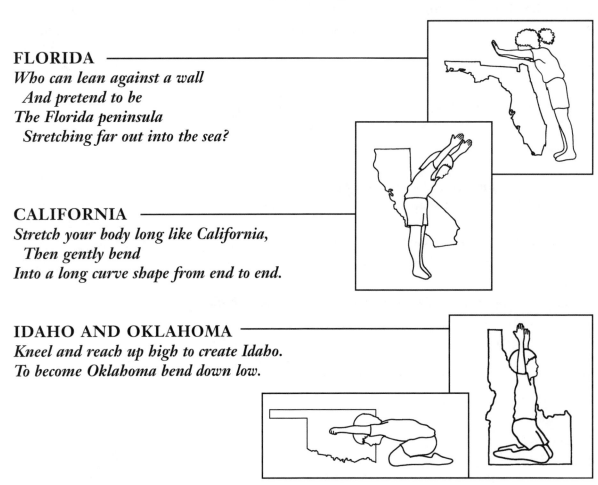

FLORIDA

Who can lean against a wall
  And pretend to be
The Florida peninsula
  Stretching far out into the sea?

CALIFORNIA

Stretch your body long like California,
  Then gently bend
Into a long curve shape from end to end.

IDAHO AND OKLAHOMA

Kneel and reach up high to create Idaho.
To become Oklahoma bend down low.

GEOMETRIC STATES

Colorado and Wyoming
  Are rectangles.
Can you bend your body
  To form right angles?

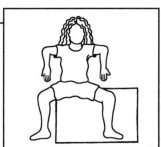

THE BAKER

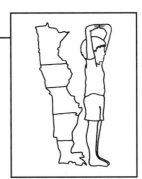

The center of the country is where he's at.
Four states make his body and one his hat.
What character do you see?
Whose body is carved by the Mississippi? (A baker.)
Stretch to create the baker's hat with your arms.
The land of the baker is covered with farms.

TEXAS

Try to pose your body like Texas and stand
In the shape of this wide, flat land.

NEVADA

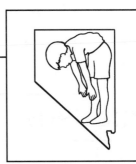

Nevada is part triangle, part square.
Reach toward your toes, and you are there.

MASSACHUSETTS

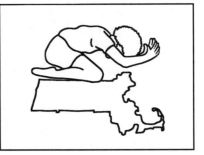

One part of Massachusetts looks like an elephant's nose.
Is it possible to bend your body into this pose?

YOUR FAVORITE STATE

Each state is a different shape;
 A sculpture made of the landscape.
Can you turn and twist and pose
 To create a state everyone knows?

MAKING AMERICA

Just like the United States, we can unite,
And use our bodies to write.

INSTRUCTIONS
- Divide the children into two or three groups.
- Encourage group members to combine their bodies to create various letters of the alphabet.
- Assist the groups in using their bodies to create the words: AMERICA, FREEDOM, and THE USA.
- Post signs with the words printed in large print to use as references.
- Combine groups to form the words UNITED STATES.
- Use a camera to photograph the children's completed structures.

THE UNITED STUDENTS

INSTRUCTIONS
- Challenge the children to form unique shapes that fit together and represent imaginary states.
- To begin, one child lies down, then the remaining children build outward from the center to create a "country" of bodies.
- Encourage the groups to draw stick figure maps to use as models for the activity and name their imaginary state.

C. ONE LAND

The first 13 grew to 50.
Now they stretch from sea to sea.

INTRODUCTION

- We move north, south, east, and west when we travel throughout the USA.
- The United States of America expanded each time a new state joined the union.
- Today, the United States is divided into six regions: the Northeast States, the Midwest States, the Rocky Mountain States, the Pacific Coast States, the Southwest States, and the Southeast States.
- The United States of America is located on the continent of North America. North America stretches from Alaska's cold land in the north to Mexico's hot deserts and Central America's tropical forests in the south.

NORTH, SOUTH, EAST, WEST: ACROSS THE USA

INSTRUCTIONS
- Explain that different regions are known for different products.
- Use a compass to locate the four directions, and post each direction on the wall.
- Encourage the children to move in the direction specified by the activity.

1. *Your trip begins in Maine.*
   Paddle south in a canoe
      To New York and catch a train.

2. *Ride the train west to Detroit*
      And buy a car,
   But don't drive it very far.

3. *Trade it for a tractor in Indiana,*
   And plow through
      The breadbasket of Americana.

4. *Travel south, down the*
      Mississippi river you float,
   As your arms move like
      A paddle wheel riverboat.

5. *Head west to Texas, saddle a horse,*
   And gallop off into the sunset, of course.

6. *Paddle west down the Grand Canyon;*
      See Arizona on a raft ride.
   Be careful, don't fall over the side!

7. *In California you feel brave.*
   Go surfing and catch a wave.
   Lean from side to side,
      Cutting back and forth.
   Ride it all the way up north.

8. *In Seattle fly on a jet plane,*
   And soar back east
      Across the country again.

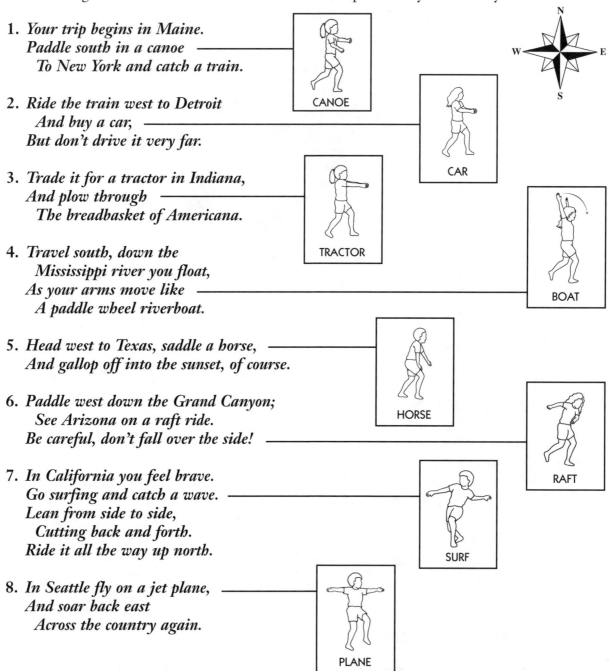

There are six regions in our country,
Recognized by their geographic location and diversity.

INSTRUCTIONS

- Select seven children to act as "Travelers." Divide the remaining children into six different groups. Each group represents one of the six regions of the United States.
- Each group moves to the appropriate location of the activity area and grasps hands, forming the region of connected states.
- Six of the Travelers stand in the center of any geographic region while the seventh Traveler faces the regions (see diagram).
- On the teacher's signal, "Travel onward," all Travelers dash to a different region while the seventh Traveler tries to secure a position within any vacant region.
- The individual left without a region becomes the next child to face the regions, and the teacher repeats the signal.
- Following several trials, the teacher asks the Northeast State players to exchange roles with the Travelers.
- The activity ends when all six regions have had the opportunity to perform the Traveler role.
- For an additional challenge, encourage the groups to perform a slide step on the teacher's signal, "Travel onward."

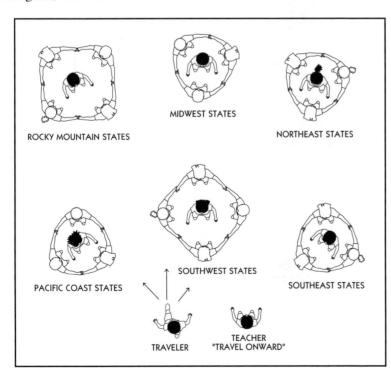

ROCKY MOUNTAIN STATES
MIDWEST STATES
NORTHEAST STATES
PACIFIC COAST STATES
SOUTHWEST STATES
SOUTHEAST STATES
TRAVELER
TEACHER "TRAVEL ONWARD"

WHERE IN THE WORLD IS THE USA?

No matter where in the world
You wish to roam,
The four directions will take you there
And bring you home.

INSTRUCTIONS
- Divide the children into four groups and ask each group to hold hands in line.
- Inspire the children to imagine they are "World Travelers."
- Place markers around the activity area to represent different countries and continents.
- Use a compass to find the four directions and place markers at the north, south, east, and west sides of the activity area.
- Read the clue verses and challenge the groups to move to the correct location.
- Read the clue verses to Group One who then responds. Read Group Two the second verse and then they respond, and so on until each group is actively moving and imagining they are World Travelers.
- As a group returns, read a new verse aloud, until each group has successfully completed all seven verses.

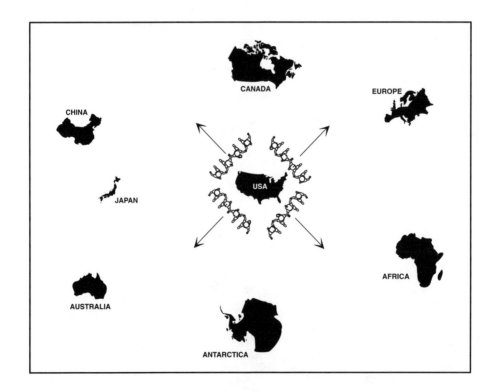

1. *Hop down under like a kangaroo,*
   To the land of the platypus, koala, and emu.
   • Australia

2. *Skip to the home of the London Bridge and Eiffel Tower*
   Where castles stand and tulips flower.
   • Europe

3. *Run like a cheetah giving chase.*
   Elephants and lions also live in this place.
   • Africa

4. *Stretch your legs wide*
   Like a sumo wrestler as you stride,
   To visit Mount Fuji,
   And grasp chopsticks to eat sushi.
   • Asia (Japan)

5. *Walk like penguins waddling to-and-fro,*
   To this land of ice and snow.
   • Antarctica

6. *Follow in a line as you crawl*
   To the land of the panda bear and Great Wall.
   • Asia (China)

7. *Walk on your hands and feet*
   * Like polar bears crossing ice and snow,*
   In this land of the Eskimo.
   • The North Pole

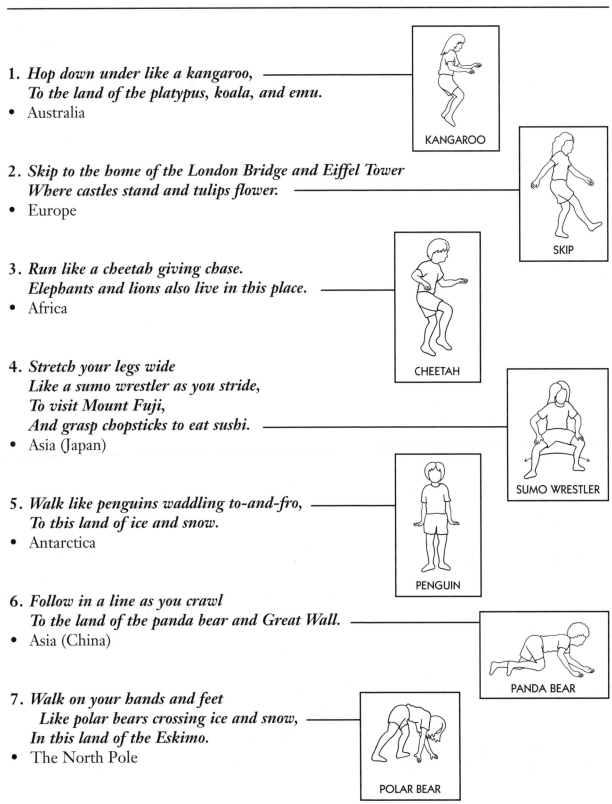

KANGAROO

SKIP

CHEETAH

SUMO WRESTLER

PENGUIN

PANDA BEAR

POLAR BEAR

"THIS LAND IS YOUR LAND"

Words and music by Woody Guthrie
TRO--©--Copyright 1956 (Renewed) 1958 (Renewed) 1970 (Renewed)
Ludlow Music, Inc., New York, New York, Used by permission

INSTRUCTIONS

- Demonstrate the movements while singing the song.

This land
- Stretch and touch the ground.

Is your land,
- Extend your arms.

This land
- Stretch and touch the ground.

Is my land,
- Cross hands over chest.

From California to the New York island.
- Lean from side to side.

From the redwood forest
- Point arms upward.

To the Gulf Stream waters
- Make waves.

This land
- Stretch and touch the ground.

Was made for you and me.
- Extend your arms and cross hands over chest.

FAMOUS AMERICANS

For good deeds and bravery,
Their names have become a part of our history.

In 1776, on Christmas night,
He led his soldiers to an historic fight.

While the Stars and Stripes waved in the air,
General George Washington crossed the __ Delaware.

INTRODUCTION
- George Washington was the first President of the United States.
- As Commander in Chief of the American forces, he helped the United States win the Revolutionary War.
- He is remembered as the "father of his country" because he spent much of his life helping to build the USA.
- A large monument to George Washington stands in our nation's capital.

DELAWARE RIVER

INSTRUCTIONS

- Organize the children into groups of four to six individuals.
- Direct half the groups to form circles holding hands. They are "Ice" floating in the Delaware River.
- Have the remaining groups create "Boats" by connecting at the shoulders or at the waist.
- The Boats full of soldiers try to cross the activity area while the Ice masses try to block their pathways.
- Exchange roles.

General George Washington knew it was time to fight,
So he led his soldiers across the Delaware River on a cold winter night.

Pushing and paddling, they crossed the river without a sound.
Into the history books, they were bound.

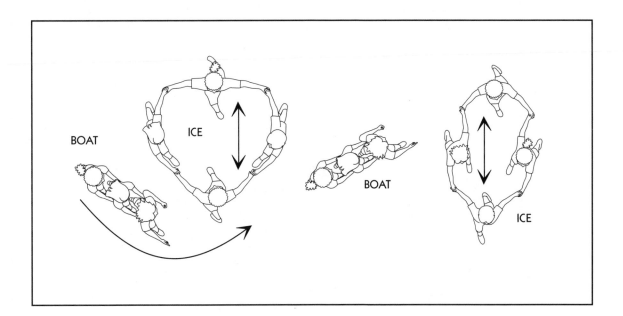

B. PAUL REVERE

The watchman in the tower of the Old North Church
Held two lanterns from his high perch.

The British were coming by the sea.
A rider was waiting to help make the land free.

He called out a warning for all to hear,
"The Regulars are coming out!" cried __ __ Paul Revere.

INTRODUCTION

- Paul Revere (1735–1818) was a silversmith. He became famous when he rode to warn the colonists that the British were coming to take their guns.
- Thanks to Paul Revere, the colonists won the first battle of the American Revolution at Concord, Massachusetts.
- The horse Paul Revere rode was named Brown Beauty.
- Paul Revere was helped on the midnight ride by another rider named John Dawes.

CONCORD, MASSACHUSETTS

HE'LL BE LEAVING BOSTON WHEN HE RIDES

TO THE TUNE:
"SHE'LL BE COMING 'ROUND THE MOUNTAIN"

INSTRUCTIONS

• Prompt the children to perform the movements as they sing.

He'll be leaving Boston when he rides.

Yes, he'll be leaving Boston when he rides.

The lanterns number two,

And he knows what he must do.

Yes, he'll be leaving Boston when he rides.

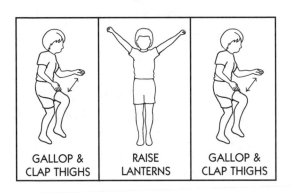

He'll head out to Concord when he rides.

Yes, he'll head out to Concord when he rides.

He'll be shouting out a warning,

To the minutemen that morning.

Yes, he'll head out to Concord when he rides.

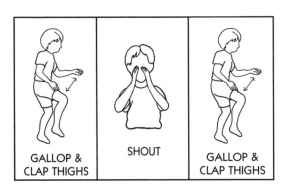

THE MIDNIGHT RIDE

"Listen, my children and you shall hear
Of the midnight ride of Paul Revere."
— Longfellow

INSTRUCTIONS

- Organize the children in a side-by-side formation on one end of the activity area. The children assume the role of "Colonists." Select one child to be "Paul Revere," who stands in the center of the playing area.
- The activity begins with all children asking Paul Revere "What time is it?" Paul Revere can answer with a set time (e.g., "It's 10 o'clock.") or with a response reflecting his famous ride (e.g., "It's time to feed my horse.").
- Together the children continue to ask Paul Revere "What time is it?" and he or she responds in a manner to excite the children (e.g., "It's time to saddle my horse!").
- At some point, Paul Revere replies, "It's midnight!" which signals all children to run quickly to the opposite end of the activity area. Paul Revere tries to tag as many Colonists as possible before they reach the opposite side.
- When a child is tagged, he or she assists Paul Revere in tagging and warning the remaining Colonists when the game is repeated at the opposite end of the activity area.

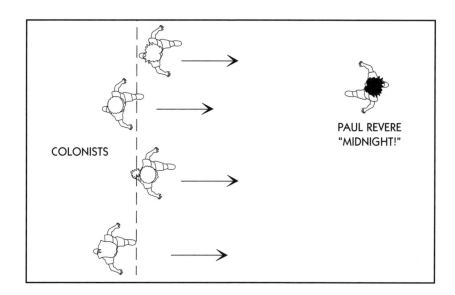

COLONISTS

PAUL REVERE
"MIDNIGHT!"

INSTRUCTIONS

- Divide the children into two groups. One group represents the "Yankees" who stand at one end of the activity area, and the second group is the "Redcoats" who face the Yankees 30 to 40 feet away on the opposite end.
- Appoint one child from each group to serve in the role of "Captain."
- When both groups are still, the Yankee Captain steps forward and shouts, "Paul Revere crossed the river tonight to Concord." The Redcoat Captain steps forward and asks, "How?"
- The Yankee Captain beckons his or her group to form a huddle and selects either one traveling action (e.g., by galloping) or one feeling or expression (e.g., boldly) for all to perform.
- The Redcoats must perform the selected action while advancing forward five steps and while retreating backward five steps to their original position.
- The Redcoats now take a turn, to which the opposing Yankees must perform the Redcoat's choice of traveling skill or feeling.
- At some point, one of the two groups will exhaust their list of ways that Paul Revere used to travel to Concord. When this happens, the group replies "We don't know. Show us how Paul Revere traveled to Concord." This signals the opposite group to select one last action that they use to pursue and capture (tag) all members of the opposite group who also perform the same traveling action to escape.
- Repeat the game by dividing the children into two different groups and selecting new Captains.

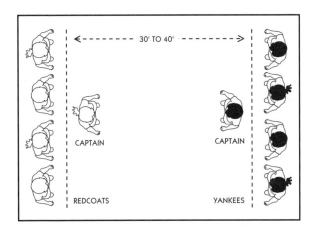

SAMPLE TRAVELING ACTIONS

- Crawling
- Creeping
- Leaping
- Tramping
- Strolling
- Marching
- Sliding
- Tiptoeing
- Trudging
- Shuffling
- Charging
- Hopping
- Jumping
- Skipping
- Strutting
- Waddling
- Running
- Walking
- Rolling
- Jumping
- Moving like a variety of animals

SAMPLE FEELINGS AND EXPRESSIONS FOR THE BODY TO SHOW

- Boldly
- Briskly
- Carefully
- Excitedly
- Fearfully
- Gallantly
- Idly
- Merrily
- Quickly
- Slyly
- Warily

PAUL REVERE'S RIDE

Watch the church tower.
What do you see?
One light if by land, two if by sea.

INSTRUCTIONS

- Place markers at opposite sides of the activity area to represent Boston and Concord.
- Divide the children into two equal groups.
- One group is the "British Soldiers," and they form two lines.
- The other group scatters across the activity area as "Minutemen." Two members of this group stand near the British Soldiers as "Paul Revere" and "John Dawes," who assisted Paul Revere. It is their task to warn the countryside that the British are leaving Boston.
- On the teacher's signal, "See the lights in the Old North Church!" the British begin marching toward Concord, reciting their verse.
- The children playing Revere and Dawes recite their verse as they run and link hands with each Minuteman until they form a line to defend Concord.
- When the British reach Concord, they form a line facing the Minutemen.
- The teacher shouts, "A shot was heard around the world," and the Minutemen chase the British back toward Boston.
- If a Minuteman tags a British Soldier, they hold hands and continue running to Boston.
- Switch roles and repeat the game.

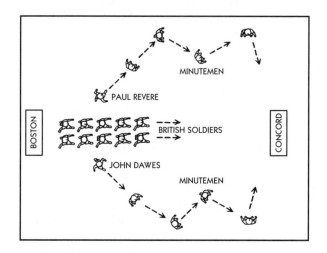

MINUTEMEN VERSE
The British are coming by the sea,
We must join together and fight to be free.

BRITISH SOLDIERS VERSE
The Colonists are causing trouble,
We must march to Concord on the double.

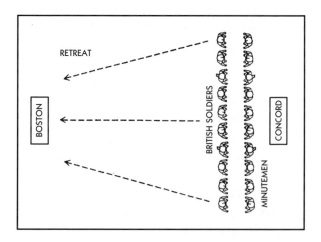

C. JOHNNY APPLESEED

John Chapman was his name,
Planting apple trees brought him fame.

Planting trees was his good deed,
So everyone called him __ __ Johnny Appleseed.

INTRODUCTION
- Johnny Appleseed (1774–1845) traveled throughout the Ohio River Valley planting apple trees, flowers, and herbs.
- He was born John Chapman in Leominster, Massachusetts.
- He wore a tin pot for a hat, an old coffee sack for a shirt, and often went barefoot even during cold weather.
- Johnny Appleseed's gravestone reads, "He Lived for Others."

ASK THE CHILDREN TO CREATE NICKNAMES FOR THEMSELVES.

OHIO RIVER

JOHNNY HAD AN APPLE SEED

TO THE TUNE:
"MARY HAD A LITTLE LAMB"

INSTRUCTIONS

• Demonstrate the movements while singing the song.

Johnny had some apple seeds, apple seeds, apple seeds,
Johnny had some apple seeds,
He planted them with glee.

And everywhere that Johnny walked, Johnny walked, Johnny walked,
Everywhere that Johnny walked,
There soon would grow a tree.

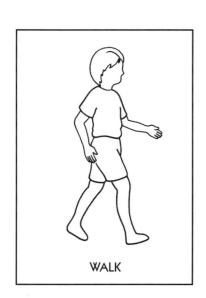

WALK

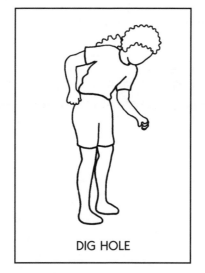

DIG HOLE

RAISE ARMS UPWARD
LIKE A TREE

INSTRUCTIONS

- Inform the children that the apple tree is the most widely cultivated and best known fruit tree in the United States.
- Convey that in 1649 the Governor of the Plymouth colony secured 500 apple trees and had them planted over 200 acres of land. The apples were one of the first American goods traded to other countries.
- Select one child to be the "Buyer," or chaser. All other children form a line and place their hands on the shoulder or the waist of the person standing in front of them. The first child in line is the "Gardener" and the last player is the "Apple."
- The Buyer approaches the Gardener and states, "I would like to buy an apple." The Gardener replies, "You will find one on the last tree in the orchard."
- On this statement, the Apple immediately tries to dash to the head of the line without being tagged by the Buyer. If successful, the Apple becomes the new Gardener, and the Buyer must try again.
- If the Apple is tagged while dodging and darting to the front, the Apple becomes the next Buyer.
- Create three or four orchards when working with large groups.
- This game was first played in the United States during the middle 1800s.

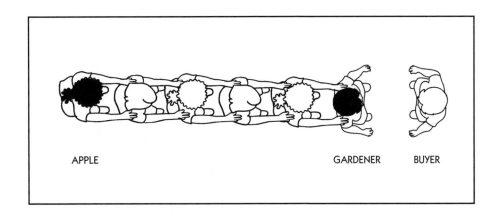

APPLE   GARDENER   BUYER

After this woman became free,
She helped others escape from slavery.

From the South to the North the slaves ran.
Her name was __ __ Harriet Tubman.

INTRODUCTION
- Harriet Tubman (1821–1913) was born in Dorchester County, Maryland.
- She escaped from slavery in the year 1849.
- She became a "conductor" on the underground railroad and led more than 300 individuals to freedom.
- The underground railroad was a network of "safe houses" that helped escaped slaves travel from the South to the North.

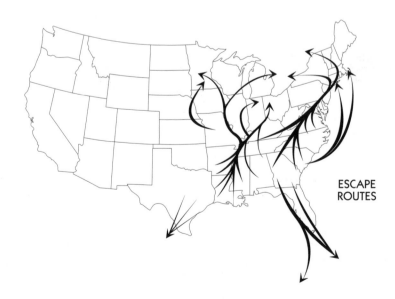

ESCAPE ROUTES

THE UNDERGROUND RAILROAD

*In this game, the partners each have a different role.
It takes teamwork to reach your goal.*

INSTRUCTIONS

- Designate opposite ends of the activity area as "North" and "South."
- Place markers 25 to 30 feet apart to be used as safe house bases.
- Divide the children into pairs: one fleeing "Slave," one "Conductor."
- Select "Chasers" to be placed between the bases.
- The Chasers recite the "Chaser's Verse" as they attempt to tag a fleeing Slave on the back.
- The fleeing Slaves cannot be tagged while on a safe house base.
- If tagged, the Slave and Conductor must return to the South and stand at the end of the line.
- The pairs recite the "Conductor's Verse" and leave the South after a few seconds.
- The Conductors help their partners move between the safe houses and escape to the North by blocking the Chasers.
- After a pair reaches the North, they hold hands and return to help the other teams escape by blocking the Chasers.
- Play ends when everyone reaches the North.

CONDUCTOR'S VERSE
*All people in this country
Have the right to live free.*

CHASER'S VERSE
*I'll catch you if I can,
And send you back to where you began.*

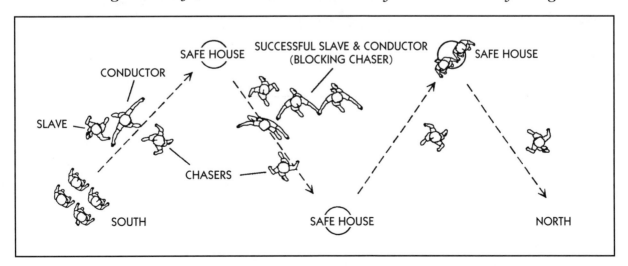

ESCAPE TO A SAFE HOUSE

INSTRUCTIONS

- Select one child to be a "Runner" and one child to act as a "Chaser." All other children select partners, clasp hands, and assume the role of a "Safe House" scattered and moving throughout the activity area.
- The Runner tries to avoid being caught by hooking onto the arm of one of the members of a Safe House. At this point, the third player becomes the new Runner and immediately flees.
- If at any time the Chaser tags the Runner, the activity is momentarily stopped while the two players switch roles, then the game continues.

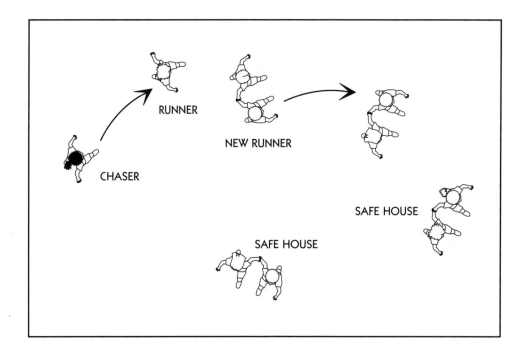

E. NOAH WEBSTER

We use his words every day.
Whenever we have something to __ say.

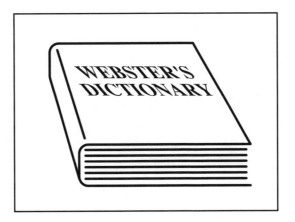

INTRODUCTION
- During the 1700s, the same word was often spelled a variety of ways.
- Noah Webster was a schoolmaster who wrote the *American Spelling Book* in 1783. It left out letters like the "u" in the word color (colour), and the extra letter "g" in the word wagon (waggon).
- Some of the words were taken from the American Indian (e.g., moccasin, wigwam, hickory, pecan, chipmunk, toboggan, moose, and raccoon). Other words were common to the American pioneer (log cabin, popcorn, and prairie).
- He wrote the first dictionary entitled *An American Dictionary of the English Language* in 1828. It included the names of objects found only in this country.

MOVEMENT DICTIONARY

INSTRUCTIONS

- Reinforce that Noah Webster's dictionary gave Americans a common language. It helped a person communicate with a friend, writing and talking in a common language.
- Explain to the children that they can use their bodies to create a "Movement Dictionary."
- Begin with the letter "A" and introduce selected movement words starting with this letter. All children should demonstrate the definition of the word through movement.
- Recite the sample sentence associated with each word. See "Sample Movement Dictionary" on page 190. Encourage the children to repeat the action identified in the sentence.
- End the activity by challenging the children to each create his or her own sentence and perform the action while reciting the sentence.
- Identify two or three new movement words daily until the children have completed the entire Sample Movement Dictionary. If desired, have them add new words to the list.

INSTRUCTIONS

- Divide the children into groups of three or four individuals, holding hands along one side of the activity area.
- Secure the class's current spelling list. Offer a word from this list to the first group.
- The group has 15 seconds to agree on the spelling of the word and begin reciting the letters, hopping forward (once for each letter in the word). Or a group may pass the word on to the next group.
- After a group spells a word, the other groups may challenge the correct spelling by hopping and spelling the word in a new way.
- The correct group advances; an incorrect group must return to the point at which they began spelling the word.
- Play continues until the spelling list is completed correctly or one group crosses the finish line.

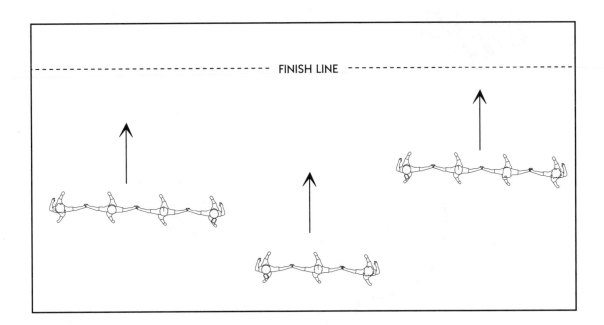

FINISH LINE

Susan B. Anthony protested, spoke, and wrote,
Spreading the word that women had the right to vote.

Thanks to her, women gained the right to vote in 1920.
Equal rights for women began with __ __ __ Susan B. Anthony.

INTRODUCTION

- Susan B. Anthony (1820–1906) founded the American Woman's Suffrage Association.
- She was born in Adams, Massachusetts. She taught school and devoted her life to the antislavery movement and women's rights.
- She never had a chance to vote, but her dream lived on after her death.
- Her work paved the way for the 19th Amendment, which gave women the right to vote.

ADAMS, MASSACHUSETTS

HAVE YOU EVER HEARD OF SUSAN B. ANTHONY?

TO THE TUNE:
"SWEET BETSY OF PIKE"

INSTRUCTIONS
• Perform the movements while singing the song.

Have you ever heard of Susan B. Anthony,

Who marched to vote in the land of the free?

She worked, and women voted in 1920.

By speaking her mind she changed history.

Singing Susan, O Susan, Susan B. Anthony.

Singing Susan, O Susan, Susan B. Anthony.

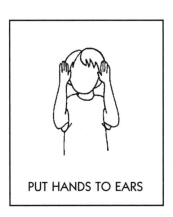

PUT HANDS TO EARS

MARCH IN PLACE

BRING HANDS TO MOUTH

TUG-OF-WAR VOTE

In a democracy the people debate,
Then have an election to choose their fate.

INSTRUCTIONS

- Secure a long, soft rope suitable for playing tug-of-war.
- Explain that we can use the rope tug-of-war activity to determine the winner of an election.
- Begin by asking the children to raise their hands to select their favorite fruits (apples, oranges, peaches, pears, bananas). Count the number of votes for each fruit. All players not selecting one of the most popular fruits must select one or the other and join that group.
- Identify which end of the rope represents the two different choices. Warn the children that they must maintain their grip on the rope or one side could suddenly fall.
- On the teacher's command, the two groups pull and try to move the opposite side three feet in their group's direction. The successful group announces the class's favorite choice.
- Select a new category for the next vote.

• Vegetables	• School subjects	• Television shows
• Pets	• Colors	• Sports and games

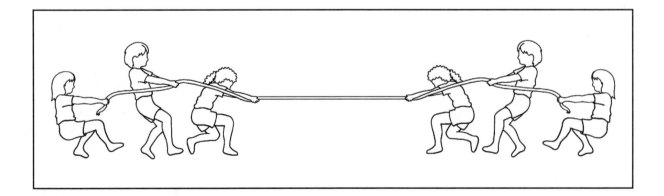

G. DR. MARTIN LUTHER KING JR.

He believed the USA could only be truly free,
If all the people were treated with equality.

He led a nonviolent fight,
Speaking up for what was right.

"We Shall Overcome," was a song he loved to sing,
A man with a dream, __ __ __ __ Dr. Martin Luther King.

INTRODUCTION

- Dr. Martin Luther King Jr. was an important civil rights leader.
- He led peaceful demonstrations and gave inspirational speeches to help African Americans gain equal rights.
- His most famous speech included, "I have a dream that one day, on the red hills of Georgia, sons of former slaves and the sons of former slave owners will be able to sit down together at the table of brotherhood."
- His birthday is celebrated as a national holiday on the third Monday in January.

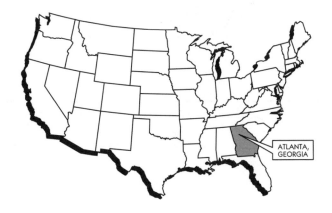

ATLANTA, GEORGIA

WORDS TO LIVE BY

Dr. Martin Luther King Jr. used the power of the word,
So that his message of peace and justice was heard.

He spoke the truth loud and clear,
For the whole country to hear.

INSTRUCTIONS
- Create a list of words that reflect the values of Dr. Martin Luther King Jr.
- Post the list of words for all children to view.

• Respect	• Love	• Truth
• Trust	• Friend	• Caring

- Challenge small groups of children to create the words with their bodies.

H. LEGENDS OF FOLKLORE

Their lives have become legendary,
But are they real or imaginary?

Tall tales and adventures galore,
The stories told in our __ folklore.

INTRODUCTION
- Folklore reflects the traditional beliefs, superstitions, customs, and manners of people of earlier times.
- Folktales are stories handed down from generation to generation.
- Many folktales were passed on throughout the USA by merchants, sailors, and other travelers. They were often told or sung as a form of amusement.
- Some of the most famous folktales include stories about Rip Van Winkle, Pecos Bill, and John Henry.

RIP VAN WINKLE'S LONG SLEEP

His beard grew, and his skin began to wrinkle,
Washington Irving wrote the story of Rip Van Winkle.

INSTRUCTIONS

- Explain that the story of Rip Van Winkle comes from the Hudson River Valley and was written by a famous author named Washington Irving.
- The story says Rip drank from a keg belonging to a band of little men, and the drink made him sleep for 20 years.
- Ask the children to lie down in a comfortable position, close their eyes, and imagine they are Rip Van Winkle lying on soft moss beneath tall trees.
- Read the verses to the children while they "sleep."

Rip slept as the flowers bloomed in spring,
And did not hear the songbirds sing.

He slept beneath the warm summer sun,
While others worked until the day was done.

He slept as the leaves fell in the fall,
And did not hear the wild geese call.

In winter as the snow fell deep,
Nothing woke Rip from his sleep.

When Rip Van Winkle awoke beneath the trees,
They say his beard reached down below his knees.

Open your eyes; it's time to awake,
But remember Rip Van Winkle when you need a break.

If you slept for 20 years, how would you feel?
Do you think this story could be real?

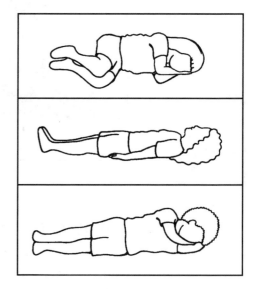

PECOS BILL'S TORNADO RIDE

A legend to cowpokes everywhere,
He roped a tornado right out of the air.

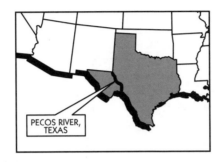

PECOS RIVER, TEXAS

INSTRUCTIONS

- Acquaint the children with the legends that say Pecos Bill was raised by coyotes, rode a mountain lion, and used a rattle snake for a lasso. His horse was named Widow-Maker, and could buck so hard no one else could ride it. The truth is, Pecos Bill was a character created by a writer named Edward O'Reilly.
- Organize the children into groups of three.
- Scatter the groups throughout the activity area with a safe distance between groups and away from structures.
- Have the children each join one hand and face the same direction so they will move forward when spinning in a circle (see diagram).
- Challenge them to mimic the actions of Pecos Bill riding a tornado and count the number of circles they can complete before experiencing dizziness.

Swing your rope and lasso a tornado.
Hang on as it twirls you to and fro.

It's a high-flying merry-go-round,
As the tornado lifts you off the ground.

CATCH A TWISTER

INSTRUCTIONS

- Divide the children into three or four groups.
- The children in Group One grasp a hoop each with one hand to form a "Twister."
- As this first Twister begins to spin, the other groups form concentric circles out of harm's way.

1. After the Twister begins turning the teacher says, "Catch the Twister!" and Group Two attempts to catch hold of the Twister.

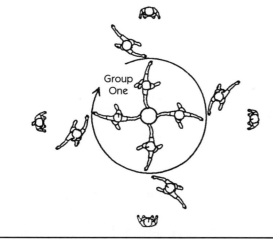

2. When the command is repeated, the third group attempts to catch the outer edge of the Twister.

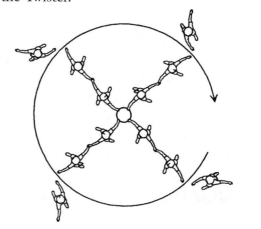

3. The Twister continues turning until the children begin to become dizzy.

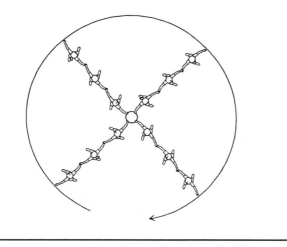

JOHN HENRY'S FAMOUS RACE

They say he was born with a hammer in his hand,
And that he could swing it before he could stand.

INSTRUCTIONS

- Remind the children that John Henry was a legendary African American railroad worker.
- He raced to drill a tunnel through a mountain using a hammer against a steam drilling machine. The steam from this machine created pressure that moved a piston up and down to drill into the earth.
- John Henry wanted to prove that men were better workers than machines so his friends would not lose their jobs. He tried so hard that he died after winning the contest.
- Divide the children into two groups.
- One group performs John Henry's actions while the second group performs as the steam drill.

John Henry's hammer rings, "Clang! Clang! Clang!"
The noisy steam drill goes, "Chug! Hiss! Bang!"

John Henry keeps swinging.
Hear his hammer ringing.

The drill rattles and shakes.
"Chug, hiss, clang, bang!" It breaks.

The race is finished; John Henry has won.
But he worked so hard when he was done,

All his friends bowed their heads and cried,
For the mighty John Henry had died.

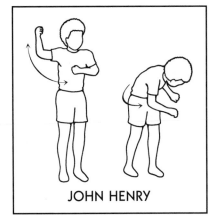

JOHN HENRY

STEAM DRILL

TWIRLING HAMMERS

INSTRUCTIONS

- Organize the children into groups of six to eight players.
- Have each group form a hammer shape as shown in the diagram.
- The first child in the hammer handle is stationary, forming a pivot point for the swing.
- Challenge the groups to recite the rhyme as they see how many hammer swings can be completed in two minutes without breaking apart.

We swing our hammer around and around,
And try not to tumble to the ground.

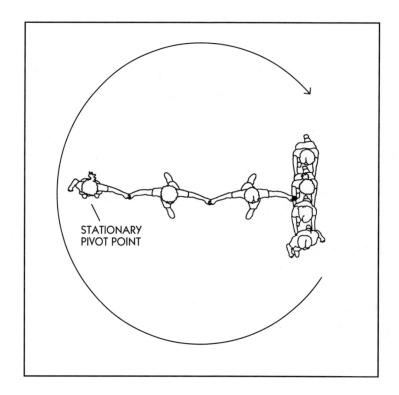

STATIONARY
PIVOT POINT

INSTRUCTIONS

- Divide all the children into groups of six or eight to create large human hammers.
- The first child in the hammer handle is stationary and forms a pivot point for the movement.
- Challenge the children to recite the words of the action rhyme until the hammers complete three revolutions.

Two steps backward, raise our hammer high.
Six steps forward, let it fly.

Four steps back, we raise it again.
Eight steps forward makes our hammer spin.

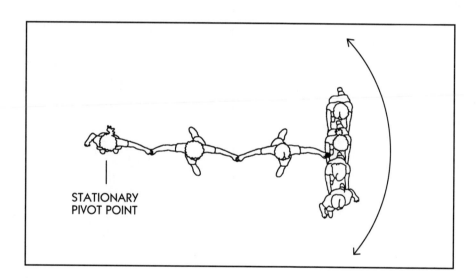

STATIONARY
PIVOT POINT

HAMMER RACE

INSTRUCTIONS

- Divide all the children into groups of six or eight players to create large human hammers.
- The hammers form a line at one end of the activity area.
- Recite the action rhyme as the hammer formations move forward.
- The objective is to be the first hammer to cross the activity area.

Five steps backward,
  Raise our hammer high.
Ten steps forward let it fly.

Five steps back, raise it again.
Ten steps forward,
  Who will win?
(Repeat.)

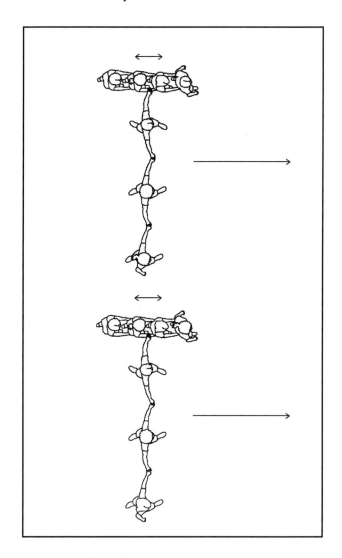

NATIVE AMERICANS

Before Columbus's voyage began,
The entire land was home to the Native Americans.

A. AMERICAN INDIAN TRADITIONAL GAMES

Play was important to the children of American Indians.
It taught them lessons about life and hunting plans.

Knowledge, strength, and skill were the aims
Of traditional American Indian ___ games.

INTRODUCTION
- American Indian games often reveal the customs, habits, ceremonies, and hunting practices of the people who played them in earlier times.
- Many traditional American Indian games are still played today.
- Some traditional activities, like lacrosse, are popular sports in schools.
- A game played by American Indian children called "You're It" is a popular tag game played by children around the world (see page 84).

WHERE THE BUFFALO ROAM

Food, clothing, and shelter came from the huge beast.
After the hunt, there was a great feast.

INSTRUCTIONS

- Promote participation by identifying that the buffalo, also known as the American bison, is the animal that provided most of the American Indians' needs. Buffalo horns were used to make spoons, saddles, and cups, and the hooves were used to make glue. The animal's stomach became water containers, and droppings were burned in place of firewood. The prized buffalo hide was sewn to create caps, mittens, robes, leggings, moccasins, purses, and saddle bags. The animal's hair made excellent rope, bow strings, and balls used in native games. The tail was used to swat flies, and Indian children rode sleds made from the buffalo's backbone and ribs.
- Organize the children in one large circle with ample space between players. All circle players represent "Buffalo" grazing on the plains.
- Select one child to be the "American Indian." This child gallops, as if riding a horse, around the outside of the circle and taps the shoulder of four or five Buffalo.
- At some point the American Indian yells "Stampede!" This signals each selected Buffalo to step back from the circle, turn left, and sprint around the outside of the circle until returning to his or her original spot and entering into the center of the circle.
- The first Buffalo to reach the prairie (i.e., the circle's center) becomes the American Indian and repeats the action in the next game.
- Create several circles if the group is large so that all children have several turns.

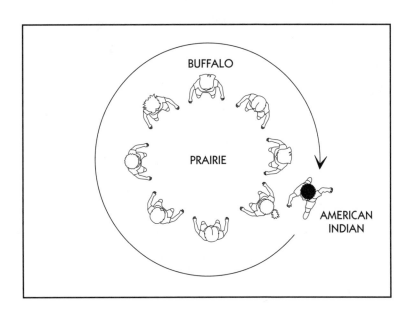

"YOU'RE IT" NAVAJO GAME

INSTRUCTIONS

- A favorite game of several generations, this activity is still widely played among the Navajo tribes of the Southwest.
- To begin, review the skills of dodging, darting, ducking, and turning quickly to evade an "It."
- Select one child to be the It. All other children quickly scatter throughout the activity area to avoid the "dreaded" tag of the It.
- The It uses his or her physical ability to rush, sneak, dash, or sprint to move up closely to any player in an effort to tag (touch) the individual while proudly shouting "You're It!"
- The previous It immediately tries to dart or dodge beyond the child's reach in fear of being retagged.
- The object is to pass on the tag and alert the other children that a different child is in the role of It.
- Create two or three groups when working with a large number of children.

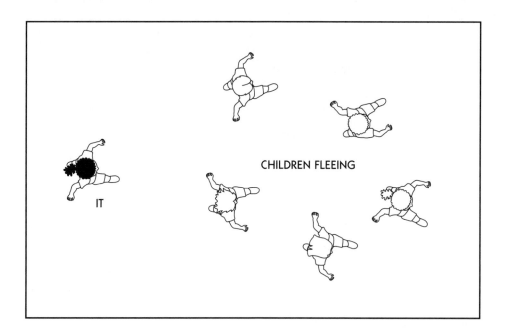

CHILDREN FLEEING

IT

WHIRLING CIRCLES

Whirling circles around and around,
Twirling in circular pathways along the ground.

INSTRUCTIONS

- Organize the children in four to six parallel lines. Leave ample space between each line. Place one obstacle (cone or cardboard box) 40 feet in front of each group.
- Each line creates a "Wind" by having the first four group members clasp hands to form a whirling circle.
- On the teacher's signal, the first whirling circle from each group moves in a twirling motion to their obstacle, twirls around, and returns to their starting line where the next whirling circle is ready to participate.
- The goal is to be the first group to have four whirling circles (the North, South, East and West Winds) complete the task.

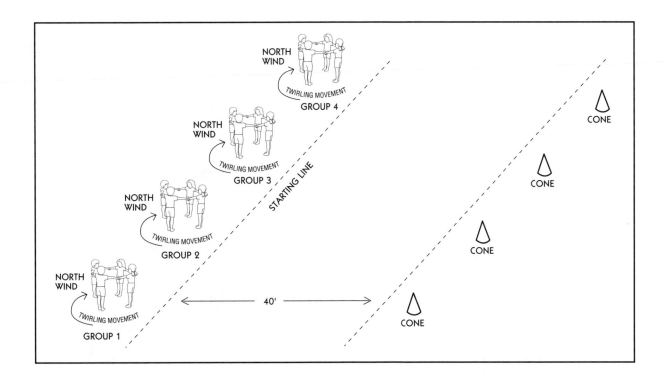

FISH TRAP

American Indians built traps to capture fish,
Which were smoked or roasted to make a tasty dish.

INSTRUCTIONS

- Reinforce the fact that fish were an important resource for the American Indians.
- Explain that they used spears, nets, and traps to capture many different types of fish.
- Select four children to create a fish trap by clasping hands. Six children represent fish in this American Indian game, and they scatter throughout the activity area.
- On the teacher's signal, the fish trap attempts to momentarily surround any one of the fish, so that the child cannot escape.
- When a fish is caught, he or she waits at the side of the activity area for all other fish to be caught.
- When the trap has captured the six fish, the first four fish form a new trap, and the remaining children swim (flee) quickly so as not to be caught.
- Create several groups of 10 players each when working with large groups.

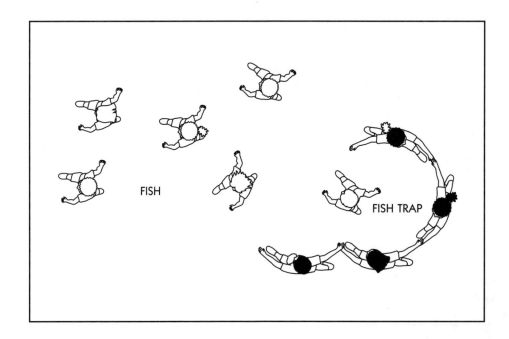

FISH

FISH TRAP

B. NATIVE AMERICAN HOMES

Native Americans built many different types of homes,
Shaped like cones, boxes, cylinders, or domes.

Each had a name that you may know.
They were made from earth, wood, hide, or __ snow.

INTRODUCTION
- The wide grassy plains had very few trees, but there were many buffalo. American Indians who lived on the plains covered their houses with buffalo hides to create tepees.
- The American Indians living in the Northeast sometimes bent young trees to make frames for their houses. Then they peeled bark from other trees to cover the "longhouse."
- The American Eskimo people were very limited in their supplies to build homes, so they cut blocks of snow to build igloos.

TEPEE VILLAGE

What fun it would be
To live in a tepee.

INSTRUCTIONS

- Tell the children that tepees were perfect homes for the Sioux (söö) and Cheyenne (shì-èn-; ān) people. They were hunters and gatherers who often moved, following herds of animals like the buffalo.
- The tepee could be assembled or taken down in 15 minutes. The word "tipi" means "used for living" in the Lakota language.
- Secure one old sheet, one for every group of four or five children.
- Encourage the children to use markers to draw American Indian designs on the sheets.
- Organize the children in groups of four to five.
- Challenge three to four children to stand in a circle, grasp hands in the center, then stretch upward to become tepee poles and recite the "Pole Verse."
- The remaining children recite the "Cover Verse" as they wrap an old sheet around the poles to cover the tepee, then climb inside and sit down.
- Repeat the activity so all the children can be part of the tepee.

POLE VERSE
Tepee poles are thin and long,
But standing together
Makes us strong.

COVER VERSE
We cover the poles
With buffalo hide.
Then open the flap,
And climb inside.

THE MIGHTY BUFFALO HIDE

Standing poles with ends crossed,
On top of them buffalo hides were tossed.

INSTRUCTIONS

DAKOTA (SIOUX) NATION

- Explain that tepees were the perfect homes for the Great Plains people because they could be moved to follow the buffalo.
- Organize the children into groups of four or five and give each group an old sheet.
- Designate one member of each group as the "Buffalo."
- The Buffalo takes the old sheet and joins the other Buffalo at the far side of the activity area.
- The remaining children form a tepee frame and chant:

We have no cover for our home.
We must go where the buffalo roam.

- The group members run across the activity area and work together to capture (tag) a Buffalo.
- When a Buffalo is captured, the group forms a tepee frame once again.
- The Buffalo places the cover over them, climbs inside, and chants:

Their home is covered with my hide,
It keeps the people warm inside.

- Select a new Buffalo in each group and repeat the activity until all players have an opportunity to become Buffalo.

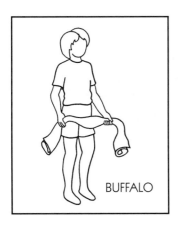

BUFFALO

LONGHOUSE

This house is long and thin.
Warm fires burn within.

INSTRUCTIONS

- Inform the children that the Iroquois (îr~e-kwoí) people of the Northeast lived in longhouses that were constructed from elm wood poles covered with bark.
- The Iroquois farmed and built large longhouse towns.
- Ask the children to form two side-by-side lines three to four feet apart.
- Select four or five children to hold the old sheets.
- Challenge the two lines to join hands across the space between them and recite the "House Verse" while bending their upper bodies and arms to form a gentle curve.
- The small group of children recite the "Bark Verse" while covering the frame with tree bark (old sheets).

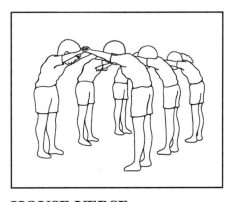

HOUSE VERSE
This American Indian home is long.
Wooden poles are bent and tied
  Together to make it strong.

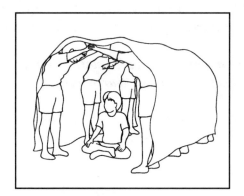

BARK VERSE
Bark is laid on the outside
To keep the people warm
  And snug inside.

MOVING THE VILLAGE

It's time to move the longhouses to a new place.
The gardens need fresh soil and more space.

Working together makes the job fun.
Moving a village takes cooperation from everyone.

INSTRUCTIONS
- Have the children form a longhouse village on one side of the activity area.
- Practice the movement sequence.
- Read the verse and instruct the children to move the longhouses in their village by repeating the six steps as they race to the opposite side of the activity area.

1. The groups form longhouse frames at one end of the activity area.

2. Two children pull the cover over the longhouse.

3. The two children pass through the longhouse.

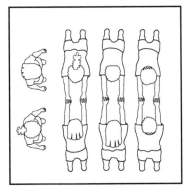

4. After passing through the longhouse, the children extend the longhouse and grasp the cover.

5. They gently pull the cover over their heads to expose the children on the other end.

6. The exposed children then follow the first group through the longhouse. The movement sequence is repeated until they reach the opposite side of the activity area.

THE IGLOO

It is well-built so the cold wind can't blow through,
A house of snow, called an igloo.

INSTRUCTIONS

- Explain that the *Inuit* are also known as *Eskimos*. If the Inuit need to camp out, igloos make a warm, cozy home away from home.
- Blocks of snow are cut and carefully stacked into a dome to make an igloo. Sections of clear ice are used to make windows.
- Divide the children into groups of seven to nine.
- Five to seven children form a circle as they bend forward until their hands touch, forming a dome for the igloo, and recite the "Dome Verse."
- Partners then kneel and bow forward to form the entrance to the igloo and recite the "Door Verse."
- Two remaining children toss a sheet over the dome as they recite the "Cover Verse."
- Repeat so all the children can form the different parts of the igloo.

DOME VERSE
Snow is cut and stacked carefully
To create a solid canopy.

DOOR VERSE
A small door is built on the side
That creates a tunnel to the inside.

COVER VERSE
The cracks are packed with snow,
Then through the tunnel we go.

C. POWWOW

American Indians have celebrations
To honor their many nations.

From across the country the people come,
To see the dancing and hear the drum.

The children learn how
To dance like their elders.
At the __ powwow.

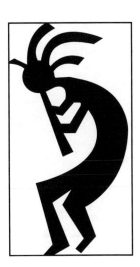

INTRODUCTION

- A *powwow* is the way American Indians celebrate their cultures with games and dances.
- Some people wear traditional dress at powwows, like their ancestors wore at ceremonies for thousands of years.
- The clothing is made of leather, woven fabric, and fur. It is decorated with feathers, quills, bones, beads, horns, and hooves.
- Others are fancy dancers, who wear colorful clothing and jewelry that they have designed.

SPECIAL DANCES

INSTRUCTIONS

- Reinforce the idea that many American Indian dances told stories of animals and special events.
- Ask the children to demonstrate the following actions through movement.

Who can pretend you are a bear
Or an eagle while you dance?
Perhaps a pony—can you prance?

How would you dance to bring rain?
Or move like a hunter stalking antelope
Across the wide plain?

PERSONAL DANCES

INSTRUCTIONS

- Have the children form groups and make a list of different activities they enjoy (playing games, traveling to school, activities at home).
- Challenge the children to create unique dances that use the movements from their lives. Suggest that each dance contain a specific beginning, middle, and ending movement. Play recorded music as each group performs their personal dance.

Your personal dance tells a story about you.
Make up a dance about something you like to do.

Each motion is like a word,
A silent story that is seen and not heard.

DANCE TO THE DRUM

INSTRUCTIONS
- Listen to a recording of American Indian drum rhythms.
- Create coffee can drums by placing tape over sharp edges.
- Challenge the children to recreate the rhythm on coffee can drums and dance to the beat.

Rhythmic pounding,
Mysterious sounding,

Toe, heel, step, hop, move your feet
In tune to the drum's beat.

Thump, thump, thump the drums sound,
As dancers move all around.

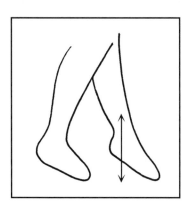

FRIENDSHIP DANCE

INSTRUCTIONS
- Organize the children in a ring formation.
- Recite the rhyme as the children move in a circle.

The drumbeats play
  An ancient sound,
As the friendship circle
  Moves round and round.

From the bark and heart of tall trees grown,
Carved and crafted with fire, stone, and bone,

Swift canoes gliding, and tall totem poles stood.
American Indians created beautiful crafts made from __ wood.

INTRODUCTION

- The skills needed to create items made from wood have been passed down from generation to generation within American Indian cultures.
- American Indians designed many different types of watercraft. These included canoes crafted from bark, planks, or hollowed-out logs, kayaks and bullboats made from skins, and rafts made from reeds.
- The totem pole is especially symbolic of the American Indians' ability to tell family and tribal stories through pictures carved in wood.
- Today, many American Indians use their wood carving skills to create wooden carvings for other people to purchase. Many use a variety of materials, including reeds, and the bark, roots, and limbs of willow, cedar, spruce, and other trees, to create beautiful baskets.

BIRCH BARK CANOE

Tree pitch was used for glue,
To waterproof the birch bark canoe.

INSTRUCTIONS

- Relate that the Algonquin (ãl-gòn~kwê-en) tribes of the Northeast made lightweight canoes from birch bark. They used tree pitch to make the canoes watertight.
- Have each child roll a sheet of newspaper to form a long paddle. Tape the ends of the rolls.
- Divide the children into pairs. Help each pair tape two cardboard boxes together and attach the support strings to create the canoe.
- Read the following action rhyme, having the children act it out.
- Upon completion, ask the children to show you how their canoes would move if they were traveling down a fast-moving stream.

1. *Paddle with a friend across the lake,*
   In a birch bark canoe
     That the Algonquin people make.

   To make your canoe travel
     As straight as an arrow's flight,
   One partner paddles on the left side,
     The other on the right.

2. *If you want to make*
     A course correction ...
   Paddle together on one side,
     To turn in the opposite direction.

3. *If you want your canoe*
     To turn to the right,
   Both partners paddle on the left side
     With all their might.

4. *If you want to turn left,*
     Paddle together on the right side.
   Paddle a people-powered canoe
     For a smooth, silent ride.

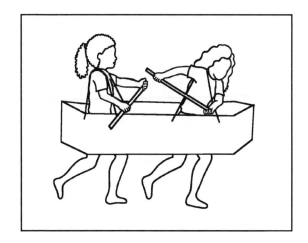

DUGOUT CANOE

They look more like small ships!
Dugout canoes are designed for ocean trips.

INSTRUCTIONS

- Convey that the Tlingit (tlin'git) people of southeast Alaska carved canoes from large cedar trees.
- These canoes were up to 15 meters (50 feet) long and could carry up to 60 people.
- Organize the children in two groups.
- Have each group form two parallel lines.
- Challenge the children to recite the "Group Verse" as they coordinate their movements and "paddle" together to make the large canoe move quickly through the ocean.
- The two groups should avoid contacting each other while paddling throughout the activity area.

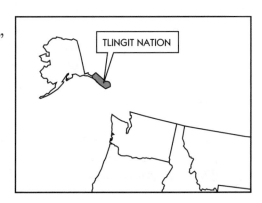

GROUP VERSE:
In Alaska, canoes are carved from huge cedar trees,
They can carry many people with ease.

GROUP ONE

TOTEM POLE

Human and animal figures each play a role,
In the story told on a totem pole.

INSTRUCTIONS

- Talk about how each animal figure on a totem pole has a special meaning and helps the owner of the pole to have skills such as strength, hunting, dancing, tracking, humor, healing, keen eyesight, and weaving.
- Some of the most popular animals are the raven, bear, beaver, eagle, whale, wolf, and frog.
- Divide the children into groups of four.
- Ask each child to use a paper plate and string to design an animal mask.
- Challenge each group to create a living totem pole.
- Upon completion, have each group use their bodies to create a story and demonstrate the meaning of their group's totem pole.

It's a special day.
A new totem pole is on display.

BASKET WEAVING

Woven of bark, root, and reed,
Used for serving the first people's need.

INSTRUCTIONS

- Spark the children's interest by identifying basket weaving as one of the oldest crafts of the American Indian. Early baskets were made by hand by interlacing or coiling twigs, barks, roots, grasses, and other natural materials into a bowl shape.
- Have the children form two equal lines alternating the direction they face (1).
- On the teacher's signal, the two lines move together weaving in and out, with one line moving under the arms of the other (2).
- The merged lines then form a circle to create a basket shape (3).
- After joining the circle, the lines move in opposite directions weaving through each other while reciting the following verse:

Over, under, round, and round,
Wound together, tightly bound.

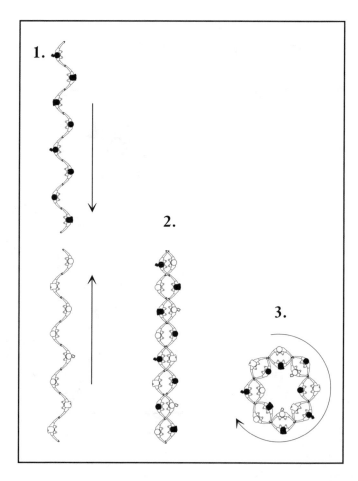

MAN-MADE LANDMARKS

Man-made landmarks are special places to see.
You can find them all across the country.

They are special places that dot the land,
Some are natural, others are made by hand.

Landmarks can help you get from here to there.
Look around, they are __ everywhere.

INTRODUCTION

- Landmarks can be any object from a tree to a building that is identified with a certain place.
- Landmarks can also be prominent government buildings.
- They can be large or small, any shape, short or tall.
- Many famous man-made landmarks are located in the capital city, Washington, D.C. They include the Capitol dome, the Capitol building, the Washington Monument, the White House, and the Lincoln and Jefferson Memorials.

WASHINGTON, D.C.

THE CAPITOL DOME

It's the House of Representatives and the Senate's home,
Above Washington, D.C. rises the Capitol dome.

INSTRUCTIONS
- Divide the class into groups of eight or nine children each.
- Begin by asking one child from each group to stand in the center of the activity area.
- Five or six additional children use this child's body to create an arch or dome shape.
- Two additional children bend and extend their bodies outward from the dome to complete the famous landmark.

UNCLE SAM HAS A CAPITOL BUILDING

TO THE TUNE:
"OLD MACDONALD HAD A FARM"

INSTRUCTIONS
- Organize the children into groups to create the Capitol building.
- The entire formation sings the song.
- The different parts of the building rise up when they are mentioned in the song.

Old Uncle Sam has a Capitol building
In the USA.

And on that Capitol he built a dome,
In the USA.

With a Senate wing left,
And a House chamber right,

Here a senator, there a congressman,
All busy making laws.

Old Uncle Sam has a Capitol building
In the USA.

THE WASHINGTON MONUMENT

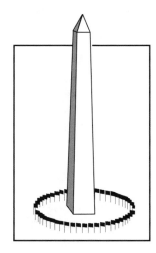

INSTRUCTIONS
* Organize the children in groups of four. Challenge them to stretch upward and create the shape of the Washington Monument.

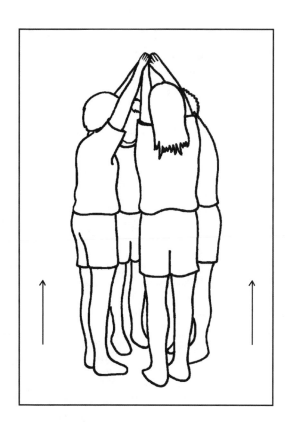

A human obelisk is a monumental sight,
It takes four friends
  Who are the same height.

Hold hands in the center to
  Form a pyramid spire.
Reach and stretch higher and higher.

Reach and stretch your bodies high,
Like the Washington Monument
  Pointing up toward the sky.

How can you make the monument grow?
Try stretching even higher, stand on tiptoe!

THE WHITE HOUSE

It is a large rectangular box,
With tall pillars that line the front door.
The President's room is on the second floor.

The people's house is shiny white.
The White House is a beautiful sight.

INSTRUCTIONS
- Organize the children in groups of 10 to 12.
- Reinforce the idea that the White House is one large rectangular-shaped building with tall pillars that surround the front entrance in a square shape and the rear entrance in a circular shape.
- Encourage six or more children to cooperatively create a rectangle.
- Have all remaining children use their bodies to create the tall pillars.

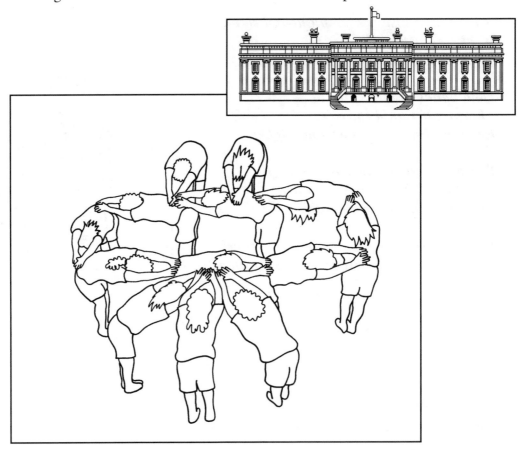

Memorials to the Presidents of our past
Are built of stone, made to last.

INSTRUCTIONS

- Obtain large pictures of the nation's two famous memorials for all the children to view.
- Reinforce the concept that we can use our bodies to make many shapes, including narrow, oval, triangular, square, curved, and diamond.
- Encourage the children to combine their bodies and explore different ways to create the Jefferson Memorial and the Lincoln Memorial.

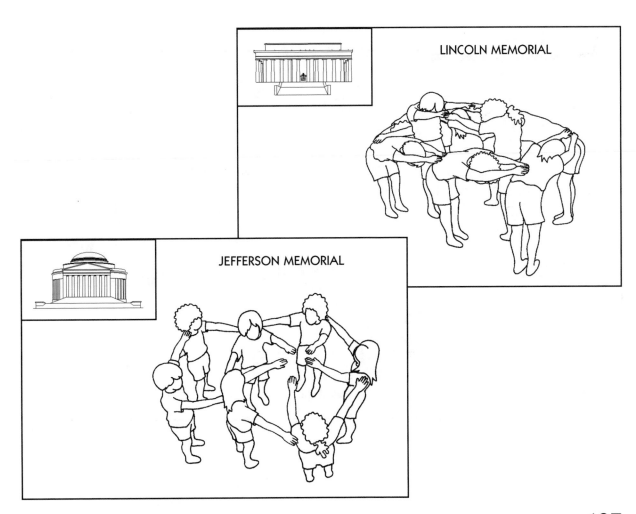

LINCOLN MEMORIAL

JEFFERSON MEMORIAL

LIVING MAP

It's the capital city of the USA.
The past and present are on display.

INSTRUCTIONS

- Obtain a map of downtown Washington, D.C.
- Encourage the children to recreate a map of Washington, D.C., using their bodies to form the different buildings, monuments, and memorials found in the capital city.
- Select sections of the poems and songs from the previous activities for the groups to recite during the activity.

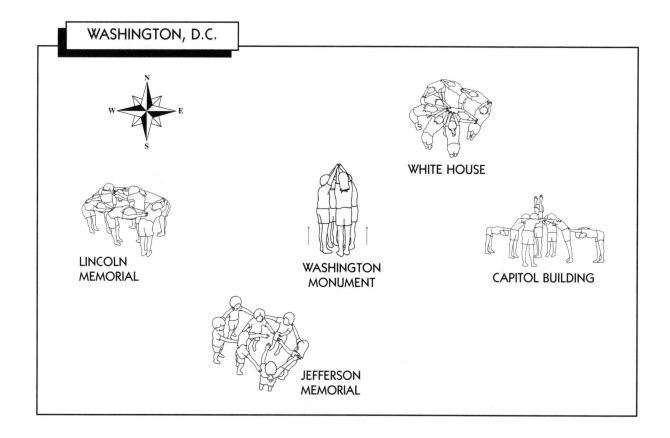

WASHINGTON, D.C.

WHITE HOUSE

LINCOLN MEMORIAL

WASHINGTON MONUMENT

CAPITOL BUILDING

JEFFERSON MEMORIAL

TOURING THE LANDMARKS

Memorial, building, or monument,
Each celebrates our government.

INSTRUCTIONS

- The object of this game is to successfully visit each of the four great landmarks.
- To begin, select four children to be "George Washington," "Abraham Lincoln," "Thomas Jefferson," and the "President of the United States." These four players stand in the middle of the activity area as taggers.
- Use cones to designate each of the four corners of the activity area to represent a famous landmark (e.g., the Washington Monument, the Lincoln Memorial, the Capitol building, or the Jefferson Memorial). All other children select and position themselves at a different landmark as "Visitors."
- On the teacher's signal, all the Visitors run to any of the other three landmarks for safety and can remain there for up to the count of 20.
- If a player is tagged before reaching a different landmark, he or she must assist the four original taggers.
- The first child (children) to successfully reach all four landmarks may select three new players to join him or her in performing the role of tagger in the next game.

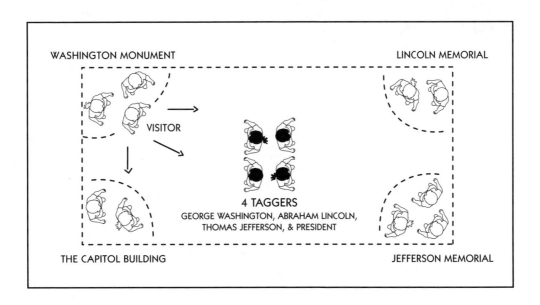

B. GATEWAY ARCH

It was built in St. Louis to remember
The days of the pioneers,
When wagon trains headed
West across the frontiers.

On the spot where
The pioneers began their march,
Proudly stands the __ __ Gateway Arch.

INTRODUCTION

- St. Louis, Missouri was the town where many pioneers began their journeys west on the Oregon Trail.
- To celebrate the days when St. Louis was the "Gateway to the West," the city built a giant landmark called the "Gateway Arch."
- The arch stands 630 feet tall and 630 feet wide.
- Today, thousands of people visit and can ride to the top of this landmark.

ST. LOUIS, MISSOURI

HUMAN ARCHES

INSTRUCTIONS

1. ONE-PERSON ARCH

The Gateway Arch stretches
  Up into the sky,
A shining steel sculpture,
  Arching 630 feet high.

- Can your body form an arch with your hands and feet on the floor?

2. TWO-PERSON ARCH

Find a partner, raise your arms,
  And join hands.
Then slowly move apart to
  Form the arch that stands
As memorial to the pioneers
  Of bygone years.

GATEWAY CHASE

INSTRUCTIONS

- Select one or more children to be "It." All other players scatter throughout the activity area trying to avoid being tagged.
- When a player is tagged, he or she immediately freezes into a standing arch shape.
- When a second player is tagged, that individual joins the first frozen player to complete a two-person arch.

FROZEN ARCH
(TAGGED)

IT
(CHASER)

- The two children are free to continue running once any third player dashes through the gateway.
- Change who is It frequently.

THE GATEWAY ARCH IS FALLING DOWN

TO THE TUNE:
"LONDON BRIDGE"

INSTRUCTIONS

- Organize the children into two equal groups.
- One group forms one- and two-person arches in a large semicircle and sings the song while the other group begins moving under the arches.
- The arches repeat the second verse over and over.
- Whenever the arches sing, "See it fall" they try to catch the players passing under them.
- Any child who is captured must trade places with one of the children in the arch.
- When a child reaches the end of the arch course, he or she becomes a new arch.
- The game continues until all the children have had a chance to experience both roles.

The Gateway Arch is standing tall
Above them all; will it fall?
The Gateway Arch is standing tall
In St. Louis, Missouri.

The Gateway Arch is standing tall,
See it fall, see it fall.
The Gateway Arch is standing tall
In St. Louis, Missouri.

C. LIGHTHOUSE

They stand on the coast and light the way
For oceangoing ships entering the bay.

All night long their lights are seen flashing.
The lighthouse helps keep ships from __ crashing.

INTRODUCTION
* Tall lighthouses were built to help ships avoid danger. Oil lanterns and glass lenses were used for beacons. When it was foggy, a canon or bell sounded a warning.
* Boston Light in Boston Harbor, Massachusetts was the first lighthouse built in the New World. It was constructed in 1716.
* Electricity replaced the oil lanterns to create a bright light that turned atop the lighthouses. Loud foghorns replaced the bells and canons.
* Hundreds of lighthouses still stand, but their duties have been taken over by satellites in the sky.

LIGHTHOUSE SHINE

INSTRUCTIONS

- Ask the children to imitate the actions of the lighthouse through movement.

Stand straight and tall like a lighthouse tower.
Pretend your arms are a
  Light shining with a thousand-candle power.

Twirl your arms around and around.
Each time they circle, make a loud foghorn sound.

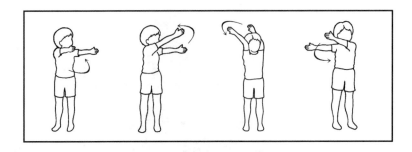

WARNING! WARNING!

Warnings come in many different ways:
Like a horn, a light, an action, or a phrase.

INSTRUCTIONS

- Inform the children that they can use their bodies to warn friends of danger.
- Discuss the need for warning signals and encourage self-expression throughout the action rhyme.

You can use your body
  To say, "Look out!"
By waving your arms, pointing a finger,
  And giving a loud shout.

CLIMBING TO THE TOP

INSTRUCTIONS

- Divide the children into groups of four and have each group form a circle.
- All group members extend their arms and grasp wrists.
- Each group must turn the chosen number of circles without becoming dizzy.

We must climb a long staircase that
  Winds up to a great height.
Round and round up to the light.

Grasp hands and
  Climb (10, 20, or 30) times around.
And see which group can reach the top
  Without falling down on the ground.

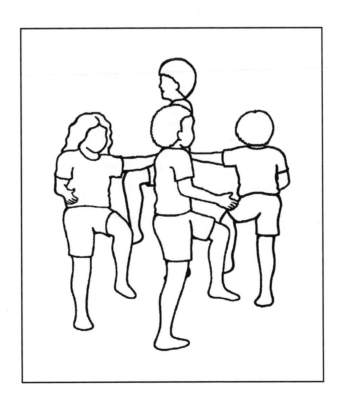

ABBIE BURGESS

Abbie Burgess was a brave young lass
Who kept the lighthouse burning so ships could safely pass.

INSTRUCTIONS

- Read the story *Keep the Lights Burning, Abbie.* It is a true story about a young girl named Abbie Burgess who keeps her father's lighthouse lamp burning during a storm while he is gone.
- Organize the children into a large circle of "Lighthouses." Place a marker in the center to represent the oil.
- Select four to six individuals to become "Abbies."
- All Abbie players light the Lighthouses by running around each one three times and then tapping them on the shoulder.
- After a Lighthouse is lit, he or she begins chanting the "Lighthouse Song."
- The Abbie must return to the center of the circle to get more oil before lighting the next Lighthouse.
- Once lit, each Lighthouse turns his or her upper body and arms in large, slow circles until he or she has completed 10 revolutions.
- The Lighthouses raise one finger for each turn so the Abbies can see when they are running low on oil.
- The Abbies try to keep all the Lighthouses burning for three minutes.
- If a Lighthouse runs out of oil before being refilled, he or she stops turning until the game is over.
- Select new Abbies and repeat the activity.

LIGHTHOUSE SONG
Around and around and around we spin,
  A light for ships at sea.
Turning, turning, turning,
  Thanks to Abbie.

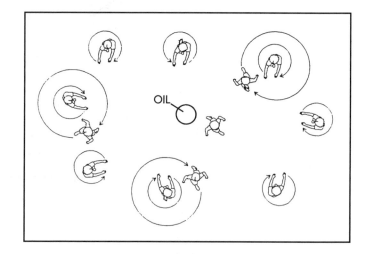

D. BRIDGES

A structure that crosses rivers and streams,
Held up with steel, wood, concrete, cables, or beams.

Across valleys, they span from ridge to ridge.
How often do you travel across a __ bridge?

INTRODUCTION
- The earliest bridges were made of natural materials–an arch of rock or tree trunks laid across a stream.
- In 1870, Americans began using steel to build bridges, which could hold great weight.
- Different types of bridges include suspension, arch, truss, and girder.
- Some famous bridges include the Brooklyn Bridge, the Golden Gate Bridge, and the George Washington Bridge.

PARTNER BODY BRIDGES

Bridges can lift, draw, swing, or float.
Some can move for a passing boat.

Grasp hands as you face a friend.
Then move apart until your bodies bend.

INSTRUCTIONS
- Ask the children to select partners.
- Challenge the children to demonstrate the action words through movement.

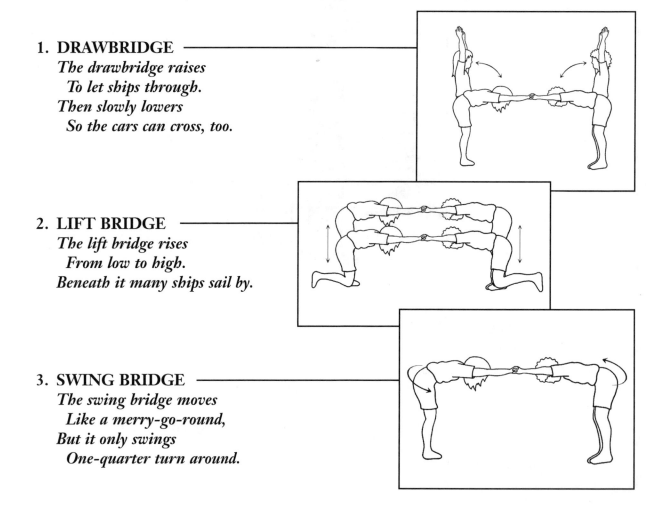

1. **DRAWBRIDGE**
   The drawbridge raises
     To let ships through.
   Then slowly lowers
     So the cars can cross, too.

2. **LIFT BRIDGE**
   The lift bridge rises
     From low to high.
   Beneath it many ships sail by.

3. **SWING BRIDGE**
   The swing bridge moves
     Like a merry-go-round,
   But it only swings
     One-quarter turn around.

THE GOLDEN GATE BRIDGE

This famous suspension bridge stands tall;
So big it makes cars seem small.

With two tall towers standing straight,
Strong cables suspend the Golden Gate.

INSTRUCTIONS

- Secure two long jump ropes or four short jump ropes per group.
- Divide the children into groups of eight.
- Assist each group in creating the shape of the Golden Gate Bridge.
- Give all children the opportunity to take part.

It takes eight children to create
A bridge that looks like the Golden Gate.

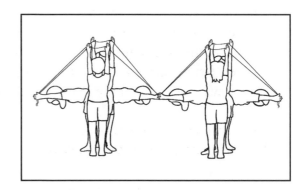

ENGINEERS

Bridge designs are carefully planned
For the location where they stand.

Some designs are wide and tall.
Others are narrow and small.

INSTRUCTIONS

- Divide the children into groups of five or six.
- Give each child the opportunity to perform the role of engineer by shaping his or her classmate's bodies to create a bridge.

RAGING RIVERS

A mighty flood is on the way,
The raging rivers will wash bridges away!

INSTRUCTIONS
- Select two children to be the "Raging Rivers." These children stand on opposite sides of the activity area.
- The remainder of the children scatter throughout the activity area and form partner-bridge shapes with their bodies.
- At the teacher's command, "Raging rivers!" the Rivers move under the Bridges.
- As each Bridge is swept away, the two players follow the River to the next Bridge.
- Play continues until all the Bridges are swept away by the Rivers.

Down the river the bridges go,
Following along with the floodwater's flow.

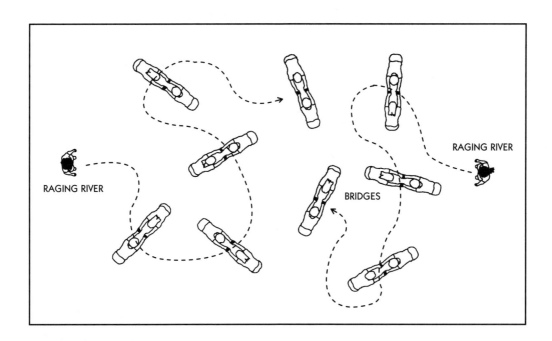

E. CITY SKYLINE

Tall buildings of different heights,
Cities have high reaching sights.

Flashing lights and neon signs
Color the night of a __ __ city skyline.

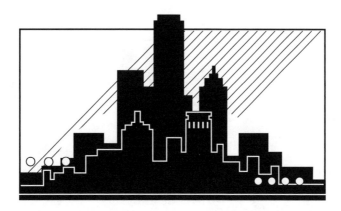

INTRODUCTION
*   Buildings of different sizes and shapes stand together to form a city.
*   There are office buildings, store fronts, hotels, and factories.
*   Some are tall with pointed tops, and others are square like building blocks.
*   The outline of the shapes creates a skyline. Many people can identify a specific city by its skyline in a photograph.

FAMOUS BUILDINGS

INSTRUCTIONS
- Obtain pictures of the buildings identified below and encourage the children to form the shape of each building with their bodies while reciting the verses.

1. **THE SPACE NEEDLE**
   Seattle has a far-out sight:
   The Space Needle looks like it could take flight.
   (Seattle, Washington.)
   - Create a thin needle shape with your body.

2. **THE EMPIRE STATE BUILDING**
   This tall building became a hit,
   When King Kong climbed on it.
   (New York, New York.)
   - Stretch your bodies upward into the sky.

3. **THE TRANSAMERICA BUILDING**
   No other building in San Francisco is higher
   Than the Transamerica Spire.
   (San Francisco, California.)
   - Can you create a pyramid shape with a partner?

4. **SEARS TOWER**
   A monument to human engineering power,
   Tallest of them all, the Sears Tower.
   (Chicago, Illinois.)
   - Form groups of four to create the Sears Tower.

5. **THE WORLD TRADE CENTER**
   Twin towers stand side by side
   With offices for countries worldwide.
   (New York, New York.)
   - How quickly can you form a group of four and create a matching pair of towers?

CONSTRUCTION WORKERS

INSTRUCTIONS

- Select three children to be "Construction Workers."
- The remaining children are "Building Materials" and scatter throughout the activity area.
- At the teacher's command, the Building Materials recite the following chant and flee from the Construction Workers.

Steel, glass, wood,
  And stone are we.
You must catch us
  To build your city.

- When a Construction Worker tags a Building Material the worker leads the individual to a designated area and positions his or her body in the shape of a skyscraper.
- The action continues as all of the children's bodies are linked together to create a make-believe city.
- Upon completion, the Construction Workers admire their creation and recite the following verse:

With rivet, cement,
  Hammer, and nail,
We built our fine city
  And did not fail.

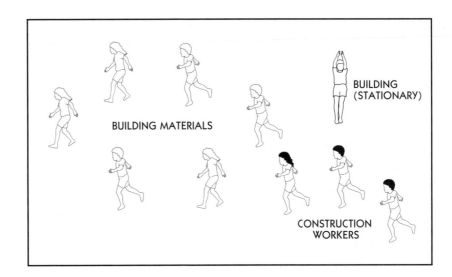

BODY BUILDINGS

INSTRUCTIONS
- Remind the children of the different shapes the body can make (round, oval, narrow, small, tall, twisted, triangle, box, square, thin, pointed, wide, angular, curved, rectangle, flat, long, curled, crooked, straight, and diamond shapes).
- Challenge the children to create individual, partner, and group building shapes.

Use your body to create a building shape.
All together you form a city landscape.

Reach, stretch, and bend,
Then work together with a friend.

CITY OF MIRRORS

City buildings reflect one another.
The tall glass walls mirror each other.

INSTRUCTIONS
- Divide the children into two side-by-side lines, facing each other.
- Ask one group to create a city skyline of building shapes and challenge the other group to mirror the shapes.
- Switch roles.
- Direct the children's attention to the different skyline views they see each day.

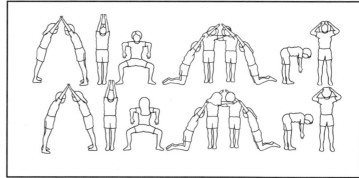

NATURAL WONDERS

Scenic grandeur for all to see,
Creations of nature's artistry.

A. PLACES OF BEAUTY

Places of beauty can be found from sea to shining sea,
They are America's natural __ legacy.

INTRODUCTION
- The USA has a diverse landscape.
- Tall mountains, vast prairies, long coastlines, spacious lakes, waterfalls, twisting rivers, and expansive deserts belong to us all.
- Many special places have been preserved as national parks and wilderness areas.
- Millions of people from around the world travel to the USA to see our many places of beauty.

THE GREAT LAKES

Five lakes connected, a sight to see:
Superior, Huron, Michigan, Ontario, and Erie.

INSTRUCTIONS

- Locate the five Great Lakes on a map. Explain that together, the Great Lakes are the largest body of fresh water in the world. They also create the largest inland waterway.
- Ask the children to hold hands and form the shape of Lake Superior.
- The child at the west end moves toward the center pulling the lake inside itself.
- When the child and the children following reach the east end of the lake, they pass through the circle, pulling everyone along and creating the next lake.
- Repeat the activity until all the lakes are created.

1. *The first lake is to the west,*
   Superior is longer and deeper than the rest.

2. *Lake Michigan is in a teardrop shape*
   That stretches south across the landscape.

3. *Huron is wide and flat.*
   It is shaped like an angry cat.

4. *The next step toward the sea*
   Is the fourth lake–Lake Erie.

5. *Over Niagara Falls we go,*
   Then into the final lake we flow.
   It is named Ontario.

6. *Finally, down the St. Lawrence River the water flows free*
   Out to the sea.

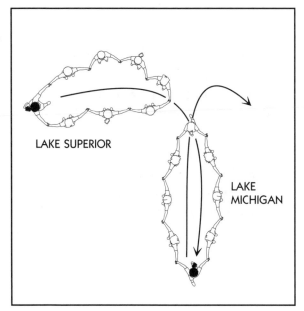

LAKE SUPERIOR

LAKE MICHIGAN

SCENIC GEOGRAPHY

INSTRUCTIONS
- Tell the children that we can learn about different places in the USA by using our bodies.
- Point to the location of each area on a map.

1. *Show me how erosion*
   Makes mountains change.
   Use your bodies to create the rolling
   Mountains of the Appalachian range.

2. *Move your bodies like the Mississippi,*
   Twisting, turning, toward the sea.

3. *In the desert, many different cactus*
   Can be found.
   The barrel cactus is short and round.
   Bend down close to the ground.

4. *The Grand Canyon's river has deep halls.*
   Lie on your back and raise your arms
   And legs to create the canyon walls.

1

APPALACHIAN MOUNTAINS

2

MISSISSIPPI RIVER

3

CACTUS

4

GRAND CANYON

5. *In Yellowstone National Park,*
   See Old Faithful blow!
   Show me how the geyser puts on a
   Spectacular show.

6. *The Rocky Mountain peaks pierce the sky.*
   Find a partner, then reach and stretch
   Your bodies high.

7. *The Cascade Mountains are fiery*
   Beneath deep glaciers of ice and snow.
   Create mighty volcanoes,
   Then show me how they blow.

8. *Waves curl and crash with a steady roar.*
   Imagine your bodies are waves
   Washing the Pacific shore.

5 OLD FAITHFUL

6 ROCKY MOUNTAINS

7 CASCADE VOLCANO

8 OCEAN WAVE

"AMERICA THE BEAUTIFUL"

MOVING TO THE MUSIC

INSTRUCTIONS

- "America the Beautiful" was written by Katherine Lee Bates.
- It was inspired by the view she experienced atop Pikes Peak, close to Colorado Springs, Colorado.
- Ask the children to perform special movements to the words of "America the Beautiful."

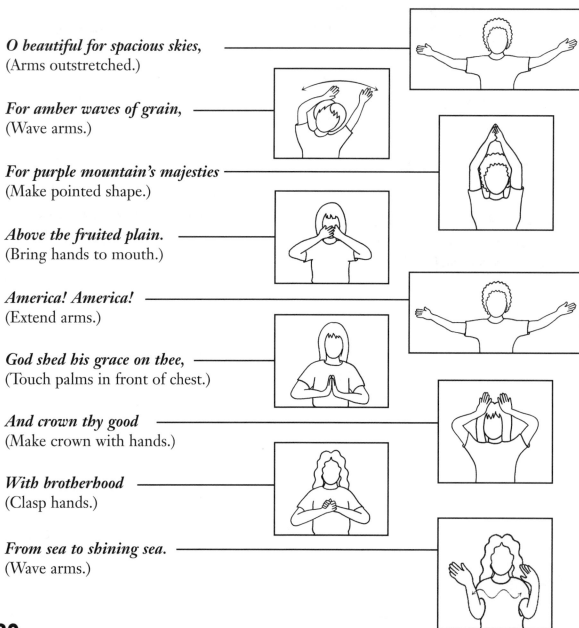

O beautiful for spacious skies,
(Arms outstretched.)

For amber waves of grain,
(Wave arms.)

For purple mountain's majesties
(Make pointed shape.)

Above the fruited plain.
(Bring hands to mouth.)

America! America!
(Extend arms.)

God shed his grace on thee,
(Touch palms in front of chest.)

And crown thy good
(Make crown with hands.)

With brotherhood
(Clasp hands.)

From sea to shining sea.
(Wave arms.)

B. THE GRAND CANYON

Across northern Arizona it lies,
A grand sight for the eyes.

A deep gorge in the land,
Carved by Nature's hand.

A place of towering walls, narrow, and steep.
A national park over 200 miles long and one mile deep.

An amazing natural phenomenon,
The wondrous — — Grand Canyon.

INTRODUCTION

*   The Grand Canyon is more than 1.6 kilometers (1 mile) deep.
*   It is the largest gorge in the world: 445 kilometers (277 miles) long and an average of 16 kilometers (10 miles) wide.
*   It is known for its dull red, pink, and chocolate-brown color.
*   It took the Colorado River one million years to create the Grand Canyon.

GRAND CANYON, ARIZONA

GRAND CANYON RIDE

INSTRUCTIONS

- Divide the children into groups of six and have them pretend they are paddling a raft as as you read the verse aloud.

1. **THE ADVENTURE BEGINS**
   The Grand Canyon is like a giant waterslide,
   A wild 200-mile ride.

   Strap on your life jacket, secure it tight
   And begin to paddle with all your might.

2. **RAPIDS**
   The water begins to make a deafening sound,
   As white-capped waves splash all around.

   It feels like a roller-coaster ride
   As the raft shoots up, down, and side to side.

   Wild waves crash over your head.
   Oh no! See that whirlpool
     Straight ahead!

3. **WHIRLPOOL**
   Suddenly the raft overturns!
   The whirlpool spins you around
     As the water churns.

4. **SWIM FOR YOUR LIVES**
   Make long arm strokes
     And swim for your lives.
   Thanks to the life jackets
     Everyone survives.

THE CONTINUOUS CANYON

Rushing rapids, twisting, turning,
Splashing, boiling, waters churning.

INSTRUCTIONS
- Relate how the Colorado River twists and turns as it flows down the Grand Canyon.
- The walls of the Grand Canyon rise far above the banks of the river.
- Organize the children into two, parallel, zigzag lines with 5 to 10 feet between the lines to create the canyon walls.
- Have individuals from the front of the lines recite the following verse as they pretend they are paddling down the canyon created by the other children.

Up and down, round and round,
Until I long for solid ground.

- Once through the canyon, they stand at the end of the line to extend the formation.
- The teacher then taps the next child to begin his or her trek down the Colorado River.
- The raft trip should move rapidly forward throughout the activity area as all the children participate.
- Alternate the type of action the children use to move down the canyon (e.g., skip, hop, run, crab walk, or slide).

It blows its top every hour
With an awe-inspiring shower.

The most famous geyser of all,
You can count on __ __ Old Faithful.

INTRODUCTION

- The word *geyser* is from the Icelandic, meaning "gusher" or "spouter."
- Geysers are spouts of hot water that shoot upward from the earth like giant squirt guns. They are most often found in regions of high volcanic activity.
- Old Faithful is a geyser located in Yellowstone National Park.
- Old Faithful erupts to heights of 100 to 150 feet at intervals of about one hour and continues for about five minutes. This is why it is called "Old Faithful."

YELLOWSTONE NATIONAL PARK, WYOMING

INSTRUCTIONS

* Instruct the children to perform the actions of Old Faithful.

Curl into a ball ————————————
And make your body small.

Imagine you are water trapped in a cave. ——
As the water grows hot,
  How do you behave?

You begin to boil ————————————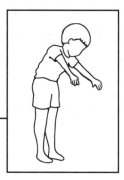
And rise up through
  The earth's soil.

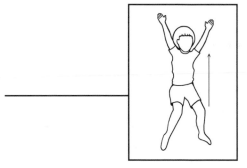

Warmer and warmer ——————
  The water grows ...
Until, Whoosh!
  Old Faithful blows!

Blow with a Whoosh! ————————————
  Shoot up high ...,
Then fall like rain from the sky.

Ever so slow ... ——————
Water seeps down
  Into the cave, far below.

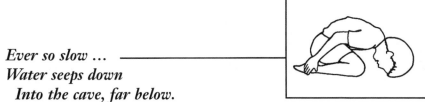

WHOOSH GOES THE GEYSER

TO THE TUNE:
"POP GOES THE WEASEL"

INSTRUCTIONS

- Organize the children into a large circle.
- Choose three children to bend down low in the center of the circle.
- The players in the circle hold hands and skip in a clockwise rotation while singing the song.
- On the final verse, the circle of players raise their arms in the air as children in the center of the circle leap upward.

Deep, deep in the ground the water gets hot.
It really starts to boil.

The water shoots up in to the sky.
Whoosh! goes the geyser.

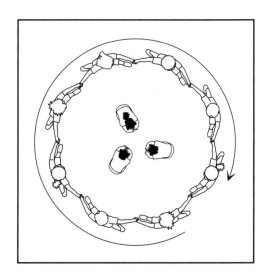

GEYSER WAVE

INSTRUCTIONS

- Form a circle and challenge the children to create a wave of "Geysers" blowing one after the other.

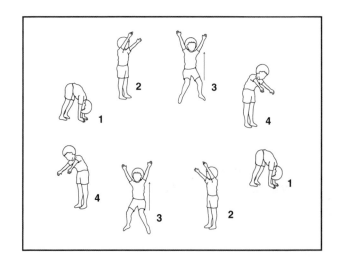

D. GREAT PLAINS

Deer and antelope still play,
But today the prairie grass is made into hay.

Now there are fields of grains,
Where buffalo once roamed the __ __ Great Plains.

INTRODUCTION

- The Great Plains is a large flat area of the central United States. The first pioneers on the Great Plains were called "sodbusters" because they had to break through the heavy grass sod to plant their crops.
- There were few trees, so the farmers built their homes from bricks of sod.
- Living on the Great Plains was not possible until farmers developed a means of pumping water from deep wells. The American water-pumping windmill served this purpose.
- Barbed wire is made from long twisted wires with sharp, pointed barbs to stop animals from reaching crops. This invention made it possible to fence the wild prairies where there were no trees to build wood fences.

THE GREAT PLAINS

PRAIRIE POSTURES

INSTRUCTIONS

• Instruct the children to scatter throughout the activity area and have them perform movements representing the prairie.

1. **WIDE FLAT PLAINS**
   Lie down and stretch out
   So your body is very flat,
   Like the Great Plains,
   A wide, grassy mat.

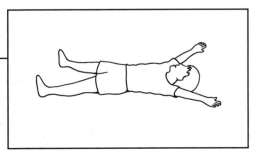

2. **PRAIRIE GRASS**
   Raise your arms like the tall grass
   Blown by the wind from side to side,
   Like the waves of an ocean tide.

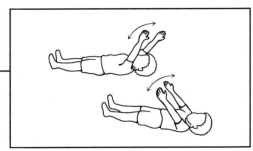

3. **PRAIRIE BREEZE**
   Lower your arms, then wave your legs
   By bending your knees.
   Imagine they are being
   Blown by a prairie breeze.

4. **WAVES OF GRAIN**
   Try to wave your
   Arms and legs at the same time,
   Like a field of grain
   In the summertime.

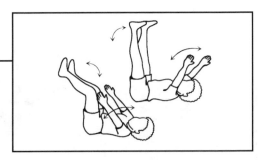

FENCING THE GREAT PLAINS

Across the plains barbed wire rolled
As the vast prairie was bought and sold.

INSTRUCTIONS

- Identify how farmers stretched barbed wire across the Great Plains to protect their crops. Barbed wire was purchased in large, round rolls called "bundles."
- Tell the children to hold hands and form a circle in one corner of the activity area to represent a roll of barbed wire.
- Challenge them to unroll the wire to create a fence, then roll it up again from the opposite end.
- Repeat the movement sequence until the entire activity area has been fenced.

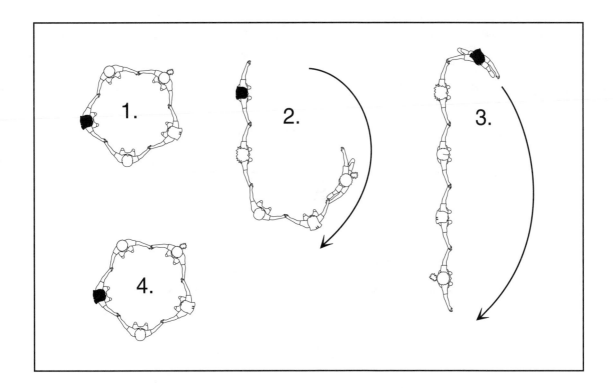

JUMP THE FENCE

Foxes, bobcats, coyotes, deer, and bear
All wanted the farmers to share.

INSTRUCTIONS

- Position a series of cones or several two-by-four-inch planks to create a long fence. Use a long rope if no other equipment is available.
- Remind the children that pioneer families created fences to protect their crops from wildlife and range cattle that roamed the open lands of the West.
- Select one child to be the "Farmer" who is positioned on one side of the fence, protecting imaginary crops. The remaining children represent buffalo, fox, coyote, antelope, bear, deer, and range cattle. They imitate the movements of these animals on the opposite side of the fence.
- At some point, one or two daring Animals leap over the fence and are eligible to be tagged by the Farmer. They may also leap back for safety.
- The Farmer continues to protect his or her imaginary crops by tagging as many Animals as possible. The Farmer may not tag any player whose feet are in the air when jumping over the fence.
- If an Animal is tagged, the player becomes a farmhand or a family member who assists the Farmer.
- Caution all children to only jump the fence when ample space is available.

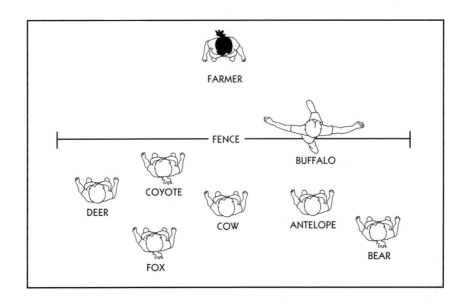

E. THE EVERGLADES

A flock of flamingos stands around.
Alligators crawl across the ground.

Tall grass and cypress trees
Wave in the warm breeze.

The manatee swims, and the heron wades
In the marshlands of the __ Everglades.

INTRODUCTION
- The word *everglade* means marsh or swamp land.
- The Everglades comprise the largest swamp in the world.
- Tall grass and shallow water cover most of the Everglades.
- It is also home to many animals, including the cougar, bobcat, black bear, otter, opossum, alligator, and raccoon.

THE EVERGLADES, FLORIDA

THE EVERGLADES ENVIRONMENT

INSTRUCTIONS
- Challenge the children to create movements that represent the Everglades environment.
- After the children have had a chance to practice all the movements, assign them to be the different objects and animals needed to create the Everglades.
- Encourage the children to freely interact as they move around the activity area.
- Exchange roles.

1. AIRBOATS
It's time to take an airboat ride.
Across the Everglades you glide.
The propeller twirls around and around.
"Whir-r-r-r!" make an airboat sound.

2. AN ALLIGATOR
An alligator opens
  Its long mouth wide,
As it moves its body
  From side to side.

3. THE HERON
A heron is slowly stalking
  Its favorite dish,
Wading on long, thin legs
  Trying to catch a fish.

4. SWIMMING MANATEES

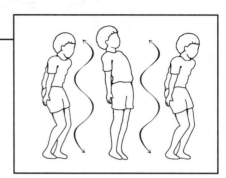

A manatee gracefully swims by,
Like a cloud floating in the sky.
Sway your whole body like a manatee,
Swimming through the water gracefully.

5. A FLOCK OF FLAMINGOS

A flock of flamingos is standing on a beach.
Good balance is what they teach.
Some are standing on one leg
  With their wings at their side.
Others hold their wings out wide.

6. THE MANGROVE FOREST

Find a partner to create
  A mangrove tree standing tall.
Its roots grow out from its trunk
  So it doesn't fall.

DOWN IN THE EVERGLADES

TO THE TUNE:
"DOWN IN THE VALLEY"

INSTRUCTIONS

• Heighten the children's interest by vigorously moving and singing the song.

Down in the Everglades

Where tall swamp grass grows.
(Move upper body from side to side like tall grass.)

Hop up and down

So the gators can't bite your toes.
(Move arms and legs like an alligator's mouth.)

So they can't bite your toes, child.
So they can't bite your toes.
Hop up and down
So they can't bite your toes.

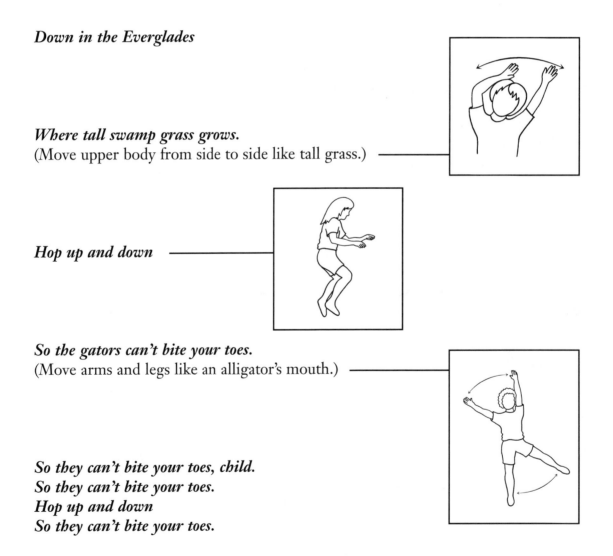

BUILDING A COUNTRY

Hard work has changed the face of this land;
When there is a job to do, we all lend a hand.

Person to person across the nation,
We are all linked through __ communication.

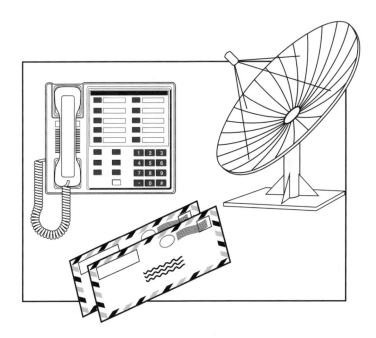

INTRODUCTION
- Eyes and ears help people receive messages. People also send messages through body gestures and other actions.
- All the ways people receive or send messages is called *communication*.
- Over the years, messages have been sent by drums or special riders on horseback, through newspapers, and by telephone.
- Today, satellites positioned above the earth can send messages and news through our televisions and computers.

INSTRUCTIONS

- Organize the children into six groups. Assign each group a form of communication to practice and perform.
- Read the following action rhymes as each group demonstrates their movement at the appropriate time.
- Rotate the assigned forms of communication until all groups have performed each movement.

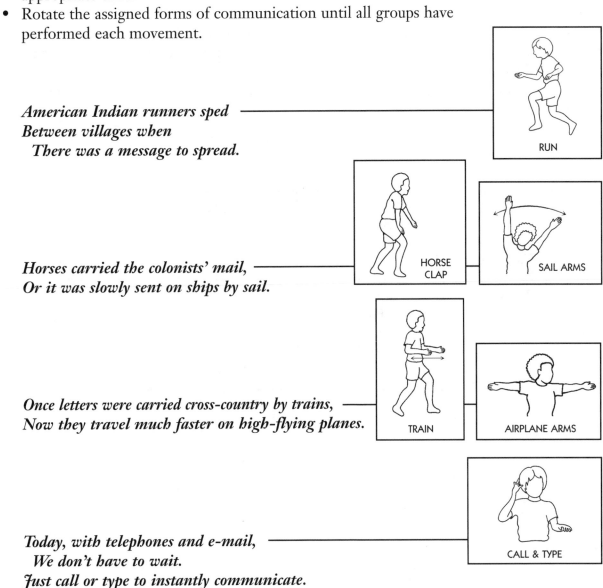

American Indian runners sped
Between villages when
  There was a message to spread.

Horses carried the colonists' mail,
Or it was slowly sent on ships by sail.

Once letters were carried cross-country by trains,
Now they travel much faster on high-flying planes.

Today, with telephones and e-mail,
  We don't have to wait.
Just call or type to instantly communicate.

BODY LANGUAGE

You can communicate without making a sound,
Just move your body all around.

INSTRUCTIONS

- Play is similar to charades.
- Create a list of action words identifying how specific people or things move.
- Divide the children into two groups and have them form lines on opposite sides of the activity area.
- Each group has 20 seconds to guess the word the other group is demonstrating or acting out.

ACTION WORDS

Jump	Turn	Skate	Explore
Run	Stomp	Swim	Slither
Leap	Waddle	Shake	Charge
Catch	Stretch	Sway	Tramp
Throw	Bend	Fall	Climb
Hop	Squeeze	Wiggle	Dart
Crawl	Hug	Turn	Gallop
Sneak	March	Push	Scamper
Skip	Roll	Spin	Strut
Twist	Fly	Bounce	Shuffle

The fastest way to send a message in the Wild West
Was on the back of a horse by the Pony Express.

INSTRUCTIONS

- The Pony Express riders carried mail from Missouri to California. The trip took eight days as they passed the mail to each other from galloping horses.
- Many Pony Express riders had nicknames such as Bronco, Cyclone, Tough, Whip Saw, and High Saddle. Buffalo Bill Cody and Calamity Jane were two riders who became famous. They took an oath: no drinking alcohol, no fighting, no cussing, and always be honest and faithful to their jobs.
- Divide the children into four groups that form lines on one end of the activity area.
- Position markers at equal distances across the activity area to represent the beginning, end, and various stops made by the Pony Express. Each marker should contain a different traveling skill.
- At the teacher's command, the first child in each group races to the first marker and stops.
- When the child reaches the marker, the next child in line follows along and tags the child waiting at the marker, at which time the tagged child advances to the next marker.
- This sequence continues as the groups race across the activity area and back again.

Imagine you are Buffalo Bill or Calamity Jane,
Carrying the mail across the wild western terrain.

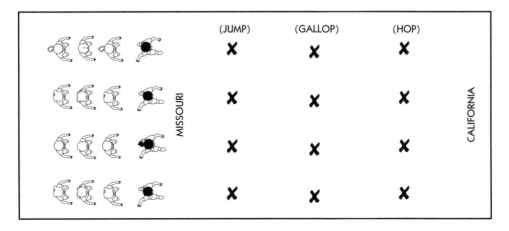

B. COWPOKES

They wear big hats and like to ride,
Wearing chaps of rawhide.

A saddle is their seat.
Spurs and boots are on their feet.

They were the tough, independent folks,
The wild western __ cowpokes.

INTRODUCTION
- Before there were extensive railroad networks, cowpokes would herd cattle from the range lands to a railroad town from which they would be shipped.
- The first cowboys, or cowpokes, were called *vaqueros*. Many words associated with the Old West have Spanish origins such as corral, ranch, and lariat.
- Other names for a cowpoke are buckaroo, cowman, drover, cowboy, cowgirl, or cowpuncher.
- Many cowboys would calm the cattle at night and avoid stampedes by singing lullabies and other gentle songs.

Say "Giddy up" and shake the reins
And begin to run across the plains.

When you get tired say "Whoa"
To make your horse move slow.

INSTRUCTIONS

- Ask each child to select a partner of equal height. One partner is the "Horse" and the other student saddles the Horse by slipping a jump rope under the partner's arms.
- Switch roles.

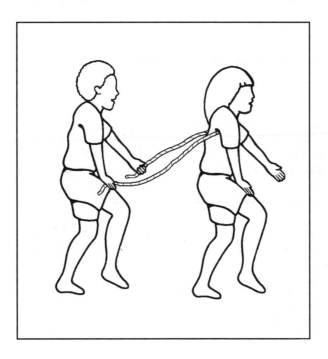

ROUNDUP

INSTRUCTIONS

- Reinforce to the children that cows ran free on the open rangeland of the West. Cowpokes held a roundup to gather the cows together to be taken to market.
- Divide the children into one group of "Cowpokes" and one group of "Cows."
- The Cowpokes form a group in one corner of the activity area and recite the "Cowpoke Verse," the Cows scatter across the activity area and reply with a "Cow Verse."
- The Cowpokes can work individually, in pairs, or small groups to capture the Cows.
- The Cowpokes must slap their legs as they run.
- The Cows place their hands on their heads with one finger on each side held up like horns.
- The Cowpokes have three to five minutes to tag each Cow on the shoulder and lead him or her back to the corner where the Cowpokes began the chase.
- The Cows that are tagged must eat grass (bend knees slightly and touch their toes 15 times) before they can run free again.
- Exchange roles.
- If possible, play western music during the activity.

COWPOKE VERSE
Ya hoo! Yippee Ki Yi Ya!
Get along little dogies, don't run away.

COW VERSE
Moo! Moo! Moo! to you.
We don't want to become beef stew.

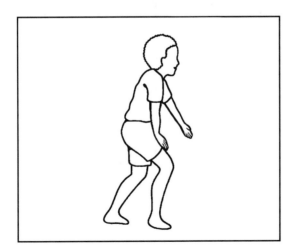

THE TRAIL DRIVE

It is time to begin the trail drive; slap your legs and shout,
"Ya hoo! Yippee Ki Yi Ya! Head 'em up, move 'em out!"

Sometimes a cow will try to run away.
The cowpokes keep a sharp lookout so the cows don't stray.

INSTRUCTIONS

- Talk about the long trail drives that cowpokes and cattle took from the wide-open prairies to the cities. The Chisholm Trail from Texas to Kansas was the most famous.
- Assign the children the specific Cowpoke roles identified in the diagram.
- All the Cowpokes form a circle around the Cows and try to keep them together as they move across the activity area.
- The Cows try to escape the circle without being tagged.
- If a Cow tries to escape and is tagged, he or she must move to the center of the herd and *moo* three times before trying to escape once again.
- Any Cow that escapes may try to tempt a Cowpoke to chase him or her and help other Cows to escape.
- The goal of the activity is to herd as many Cows as possible to the opposite side of the activity area.

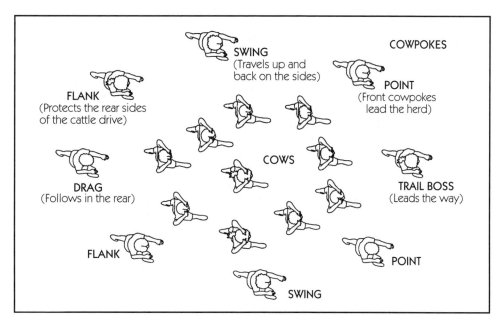

C. MINERS

With a pick and shovel they toil,
To find precious metals beneath the soil.

Then they swirl
Their pans around and around,
Hoping that shiny nuggets will be found.

In early California
They were called Forty-Niners.
They are gold — miners.

INTRODUCTION

- The first mining in America began in the early 1700s in Massachusetts.
- Mining is removing minerals from the earth's crust.
- Miners search for minerals such as gold, silver, and copper. In 1849, gold was discovered in California.
- Minerals are used to manufacture many products we use today.

CALIFORNIA

WHERE, OH WHERE, DOES THE GOLD HIDE?

TO THE TUNE:
"WHERE, OH WHERE, HAS MY
LITTLE DOG GONE?"

Where, oh where, does the shiny gold hide,
Where, oh where, can it be?
I swing my pick up and down as I work.
Where, oh where, can it be?
- Swing an imaginary pick. ————————

PICK

Where, oh where, does the shiny gold hide,
Where, oh where, can it be?
I dig with my shovel deep into the earth.
Where, oh where, can it be?
- Dig with an imaginary shovel. ————————

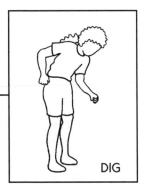

DIG

Where, oh where, does the shiny gold hide,
Where, oh where, can it be?
I swirl my gold pan round and round in the stream.
Where, oh where, can it be?
- Swing your hips so your body moves around
  and around. ————————

SWIRL

CLAIM JUMPERS

INSTRUCTIONS

- Convey the idea that miners sometimes worked weeks or months without finding any gold, while others found as much as one pound of gold a day in the form of tiny rock shapes called *nuggets*.
- Explain that some miners became angry and stole gold from other miners. They were called *claim jumpers*.
- Organize the children in three to five groups of "Miners." Give each group of Miners four to six beanbags or other small objects to represent gold nuggets.
- Each group uses chalk, cones, or tape to designate their mine and positions the nuggets inside the shape.
- When the "Mines" are ready, the teacher shouts, "Claim jumpers!" This signals all players to immediately try to secure a nugget from any other group's mine and place the nugget in his or her circle, or mine.
- All Miners quickly snatch the gold nuggets from other Miners and place these in their own mines. Action continues with all Miners dashing between their mine and their classmate's mines.
- The object is to have secured the greatest amount of gold at the end of three minutes.

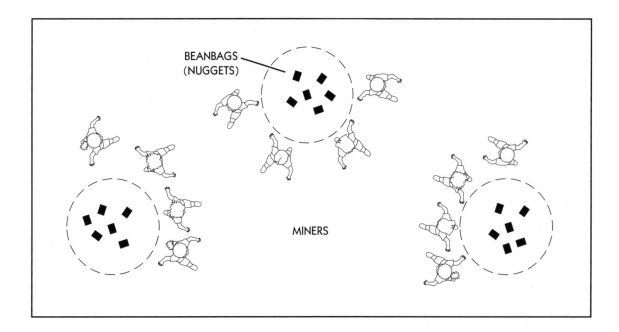

BEANBAGS (NUGGETS)

MINERS

INSTRUCTIONS

- Explain that gold appears in small quantities in almost all rocks. It is generally obtained from quartz lodes, or veins.
- "Panning" for gold involved the miner using a plate. The miner stirred and shook a few handfuls of dirt with water in the plate to encourage the gold to settle to the bottom.
- Organize the children in two or three circles, facing inward.
- Select one player from each circle to be the "Miner" who stands in the center of the circle and conceals a small "nugget" (pebble or marble) in his or her hands.
- All circle players extend their hands in front of their bodies with their palms forming a cup shape.
- At some point, the Miner walks around the inside of the circle placing his or her hands between the hands of each player and pretends to place the nugget in each player's cupped hands.
- In turn, each player pretends to have received the object. The player who has actually obtained the nugget may at any time break away from the circle, while the other players immediately pursue this individual.
- The first player to tag the runner becomes the next Miner.

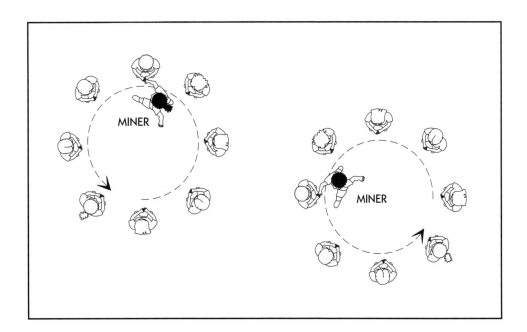

D. LOGGING

When the forest begins to stand tall,
The loggers come and the trees fall.

The trees become logs. The logs become __ lumber.
Board after board after board beyond number.

INTRODUCTION
- In North America there are more than 800 different kinds of trees and about 170 of these varieties are cut for timber.
- Forestry is an important industry in the USA. It provides wood products to build homes and furniture and to make paper.
- Early loggers used axes to cut down trees.
- Today, great machines cut and stack hundreds of trees in one day. So many trees are cut now that we must help nature by planting more to replace them.

With a chain saw and an axe,
The forest is cut by lumberjacks.

INSTRUCTIONS

- Organize the children into partners.
- Have one child demonstrate how to fall forward and land safely by making contact with the hands first and bending at the elbows.
- During the axe and chain saw verses, designate one child to become the tree.
- Have trios work together during the crosscut formation.

"Timber!" the lumberjacks shout.
It's the loggers way of saying, "Look out!"

It was hard work swinging an axe,
Chopping down trees like old-time lumberjacks.

Next two loggers would pull and push,
And the crosscut saw went,
* "Swoosh, swoosh, swoosh."*

Today the chain saw roars,
Echoing through the outdoors.

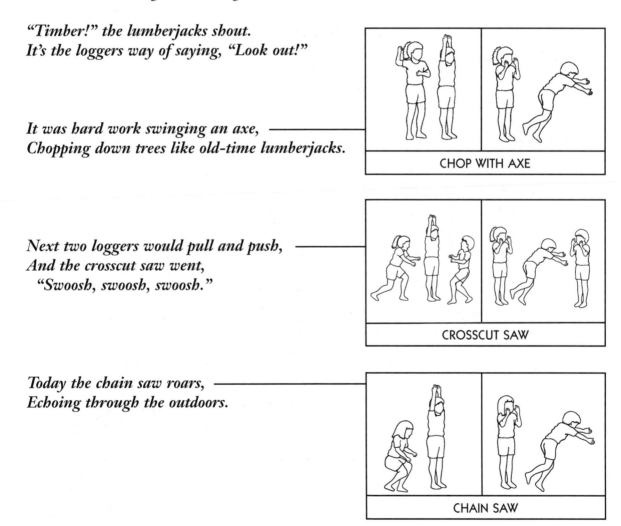

CHOP WITH AXE

CROSSCUT SAW

CHAIN SAW

CHOP, CHOP, CHOP THE TREES

MOVING TO THE MUSIC

TO THE TUNE:
"ROW, ROW, ROW, YOUR BOAT"

INSTRUCTIONS

• Divide the children into four groups.
• Each group begins to sing and move at the teacher's command so they are all singing a different verse in rounds.

Chop, chop, chop the trees,
Until they start to sway.

Shout, "Timber! Timber! Timber! Timber!"
Quickly run away!

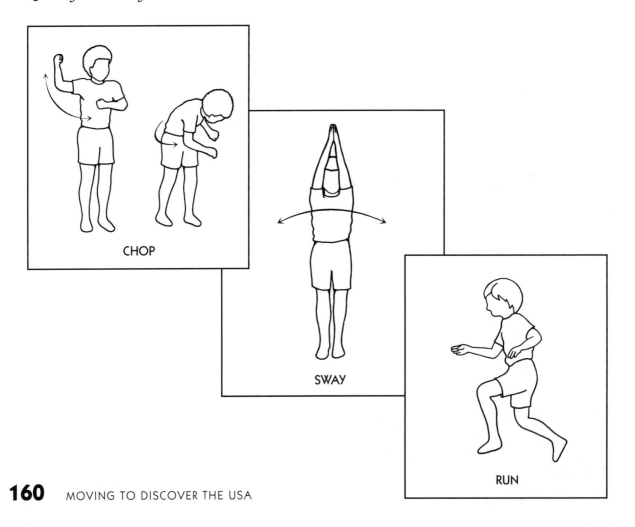

CHOP

SWAY

RUN

OUR SUPERHUMAN MUSCLES

INSTRUCTIONS

- Paul Bunyan was a mythical hero who worked in the early American lumber camps.
- Stories of his great strength focus on his ability to unclog log jams and create lakes and rivers for logging purposes.
- Increase the children's understanding of our muscles in the following action rhyme.

The quadriceps muscles help you to climb or kick a ball.
They keep your legs straight when you stand tall.
Who can stand tall like Paul Bunyan?

The trapezius muscles keep your shoulders and neck straight.
They are easy muscles to locate.
First, lift your shoulder so the muscle contracts.
Now lower your shoulder to feel the muscle relax.

The gastrocnemius muscle gives you a lift,
When you push off with your toes to move quickly and swift.
How quickly can you move?

The pectoralis major moves your arm forward at the shoulder joint,
So you can climb a mountain's highest point.
Lift both arms and reach very high.
Stretch up on your toes to the sky.

The deltoid muscle lifts your arm to the side.
To help keep your balance, hold both arms very wide.

Let's feel our hamstring muscles pull.
These leg muscles are very powerful.
Place one hand on the back of your thigh,
Then bend your knee backward and lift your foot high.

It makes the earth bloom
With fruit and vegetables for us to ___ consume.

INTRODUCTION

• American Indians were the first farmers. They harvested many crops including corn, beans, and squash using simple hand tools.

• The European colonists used horses to pull plows.

• The invention of a new type of steel plow in 1830 helped the pioneers farm the Great Plains.

• Today less than two percent of Americans are farmers. Large farm machinery has replaced most human and animal labor on farms in this country.

THE HISTORY OF FARMING

INSTRUCTIONS
- Challenge the children to perform the activities as the verse is read aloud.

  American Indians were the first to till the land.
  They planted corn, beans, and squash by hand.

  Community gardens were carefully sown,
  With wooden digging sticks and hoes made of bone.
- Can everyone show me how to use a hoe to dig the soil?

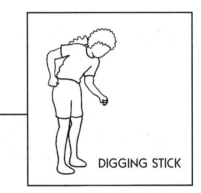

DIGGING STICK

  The colonists used horses and oxen to toil,
  Helping them plow the soil.

  They cleared the land to create large fields.
  The growing population needed higher yields.
- Find a partner and create an oxen pulling a plow.

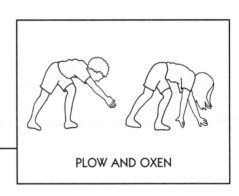

PLOW AND OXEN

  One farmer does the work of many now;
  Today large tractors plant and plow.
- Join together in a group to create a tractor, pulling a wide set of plows.

TRACTOR

GROWING FOODS

From the farmer's field to the backyard gardener,
Growing food is called agriculture.

INSTRUCTIONS

- Encourage the children to demonstrate the movements in the following action rhyme.

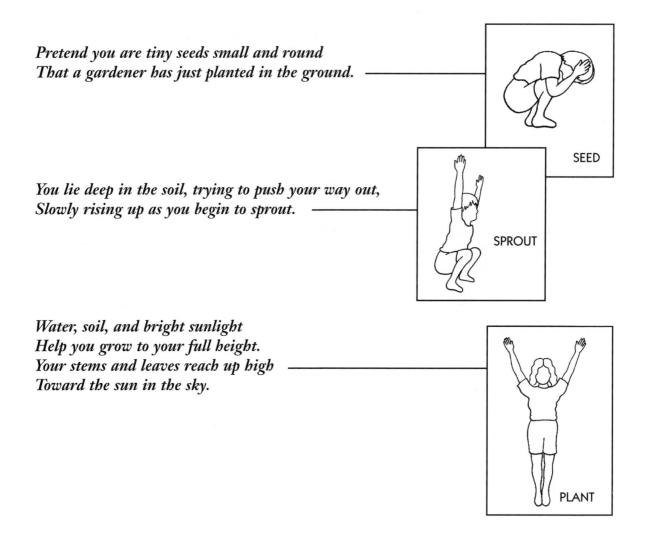

Pretend you are tiny seeds small and round
That a gardener has just planted in the ground.

SEED

You lie deep in the soil, trying to push your way out,
Slowly rising up as you begin to sprout.

SPROUT

Water, soil, and bright sunlight
Help you grow to your full height.
Your stems and leaves reach up high
Toward the sun in the sky.

PLANT

CROWS IN THE GARDEN

INSTRUCTIONS

- Remind the children that the early homesteaders and farmers had to endure the hardships of summer drought, dust storms, locusts, and wildlife.
- Use cones or chalk to create a 10-foot circle to represent a garden. Select one child to be the "Farmer" and give this individual four to six beanbags to represent vegetables. Position the Farmer and vegetables in the center of the garden.
- All other children scatter throughout the activity area pretending to be "Crows" by hopping on one foot forward, repeating the hop with the other foot, and then landing on two feet. The arms are used at the sides of the body to maintain balance during the hop-hop-jump sequence.
- At some point, the teacher taps the shoulder of one or two Crows who try to enter the garden to secure a vegetable without being tagged by the Farmer. If successful, the Crow keeps the vegetable.
- If the Crow is tagged before escaping the garden, the Crow must return the vegetable to the Farmer. Challenge other Crows to enter the garden.
- Play continues until all vegetables have been secured or three minutes have passed; then select a new Farmer.

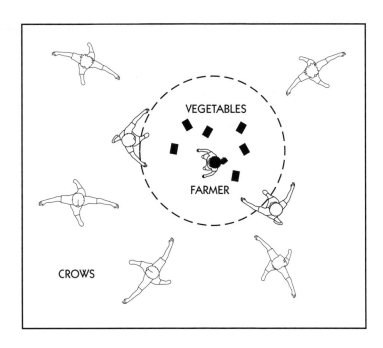

GIVING BACK TO THE LAND

Our land gives and then we take.
To not respect our earth is a big mistake.
There are three Rs in the conservation cycle:
They are reduce, reuse, and recycle.

INSTRUCTIONS

- *Reduce* means "create less waste."
- *Reuse* means "find a way to use something more than once."
- *Recycle* means "collect waste to be used again."
- Collect sheets of scrap paper that have been used on one side.
- Place one sheet of paper for each child on one side of the activity area.
- Place three trash baskets on the opposite side of the activity area and have all the children form a side-by-side line facing the three containers.
- At the teacher's signal, the children recite the first verse, then race to the paper.

Reduce, *and don't use something new*
When something old will also do.

- When they reach the sheets of paper, they fold them into paper airplanes and the teacher recites the second verse.

Reuse, *to create*
Something that works just great.

- Challenge the children to fly their planes to the halfway mark across the activity area, then crumple the paper airplanes into a ball while the teacher recites the third verse, as they attempt to throw the paper balls into one of the trash cans.

Recycle, *please don't waste the land.*
Pitch in now and lend a hand.

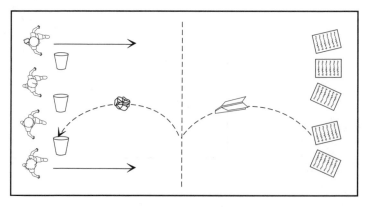

TRANSPORTATION

Transportation has changed throughout history,
As we have invented new ways to cross the country.

You don't need a car, bus, or train,
A motorcycle, boat, or an airplane.

You don't need tracks or highways:
Your body can move many different — ways.

INTRODUCTION
- People have traveled to North America throughout history. The types of transportation have changed through the years.
- People have used log rafts, reed boats, sailing ships, iron steamships, supertankers, and submarines to move through the water.
- Steam locomotives have been replaced by electric and diesel trains to move people by rail.
- Now we can move swiftly through the skies in airplanes and jets.

INSTRUCTIONS

• Challenge the children to perform all traveling skills in the following action rhyme.

Your body is ready and waiting for you to say,
"Let's get moving–it's time to play!"

You can crawl ... walk ... or hop....
Just keep moving, don't stop.

Skip ... jog ... now run....
Moving is so much fun.

Roll along now on the ground,
Turning round and round and round.

Slither like a skinny snake....
Now pretend you are swimming in a lake.

Waddle like a quacking duck....
Now imagine your feet are stuck in sticky muck.

Follow the leader like sheep in a herd....
Flap your arms and fly like a bird.

Imagine you are skating on smooth ice...,
Then scurry about like tiny mice.

First leap ... then march ... at last tiptoe...,
Then walk backward, moving slow.

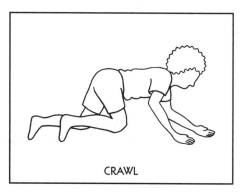

CRAWL

WALK

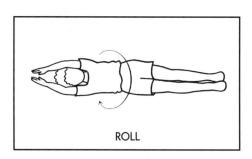

ROLL

HOP

MOVING THROUGH TIME

INSTRUCTIONS

- Read the verses and challenge the children to interpret them as they move throughout the activity area.
- Use the additional instructions to prompt participation when needed.

1. ***In the beginning of our history American Indians walked across the country.***
- How many different ways can you walk across the activity area (fast, slow, forward, backward, sideways, long steps, short steps, sneak, stomp)?

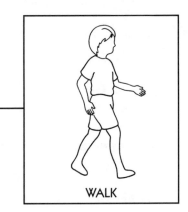

WALK

2. ***Immigrants from East and West Sailed here in tall ships, Built for long ocean trips.***
- Raise your arms and imagine the wind is blowing you throughout the activity area.

SAIL

3. ***Riding on horseback was the way Paul Revere once saved the day.***
- When I say "Go!" show me how you can gallop at full speed.

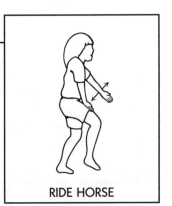

RIDE HORSE

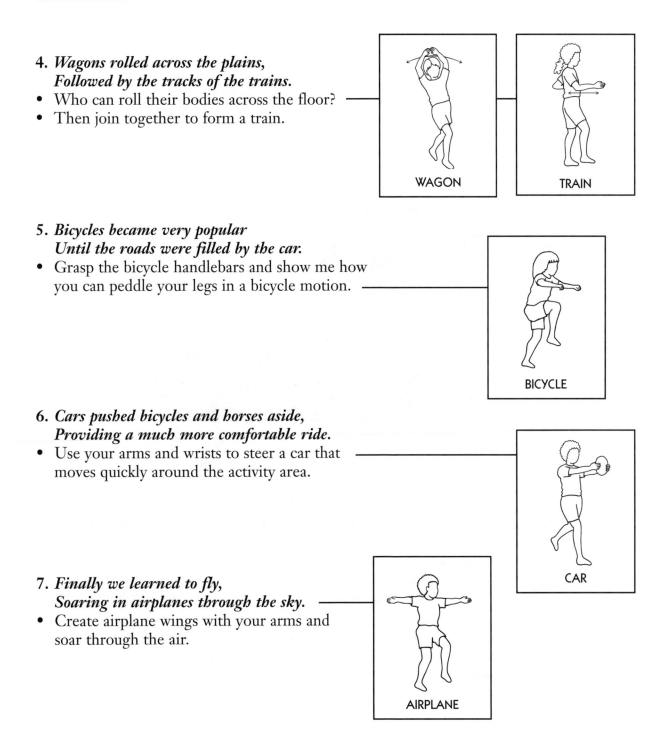

4. **Wagons rolled across the plains,**
   Followed by the tracks of the trains.
   - Who can roll their bodies across the floor?
   - Then join together to form a train.

WAGON

TRAIN

5. **Bicycles became very popular**
   Until the roads were filled by the car.
   - Grasp the bicycle handlebars and show me how you can peddle your legs in a bicycle motion.

BICYCLE

6. **Cars pushed bicycles and horses aside,**
   Providing a much more comfortable ride.
   - Use your arms and wrists to steer a car that moves quickly around the activity area.

CAR

7. **Finally we learned to fly,**
   Soaring in airplanes through the sky.
   - Create airplane wings with your arms and soar through the air.

AIRPLANE

Boats pull people who ski.
Sailors use ships to cross the sea.

Vessels large and small that float,
Have you ever sailed in a __ boat?

INTRODUCTION

- Watercrafts of all shapes and sizes have always played an important role in the USA.
- People originally learned to build boats from reeds and logs. Eventually they created sails to harness wind power and mastered the skills of navigation by following birds, studying the stars, and creating maps of new lands and ocean currents.
- The steamboat became popular in the early 1800s. It was driven by paddle wheels. It had a flat bottom so it would not run aground in shallow rivers.
- Powerboats use propellers and run on gasoline or diesel fuel.

PADDLE WHEEL STEAMBOAT

Up and down the Mississippi River they float.
Let's take a slow ride on a paddle wheel steamboat.

INSTRUCTIONS

- Explain that paddle wheel steamboats moved people and goods up and down the Mississippi River before there were highways and railroads.
- Robert Fulton constructed the first paddle wheel steamboat to sail in American waters, the *Clermont*, on the Hudson River in 1807.
- A steamboat named the *New Orleans* made the first trip up the Mississippi in 1811.
- Have the children scatter throughout the activity area as they imitate the actions of the paddle wheel.

Imagine your arms are a paddle wheel turning,
Around and around; see the water churning.

Breathe deep and scoop the water.
* As you reach down low,*
Then rise up, breathe out
* And let your whistle blow: "To-o-o-ot!"*

TAKE A TRIP ON A SHIP

INSTRUCTIONS
- Read the verses and ask the children to perform the actions.

1. *The simplest type of boat is a raft.*
   Long poles are used to push this craft.
- Reach up high and grasp an imaginary pole, then push downward to move the raft.

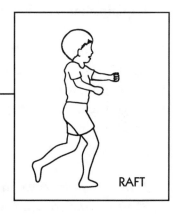

RAFT

2. *You need to paddle on one side,*
   To go on an American Indian canoe ride.
- Kneel on the floor and paddle your canoe.

PADDLE

3. *Use each arm to pull an oar,*
   As you row a boat away from shore.
- Sit down, then reach forward and pull the oars toward your chest.

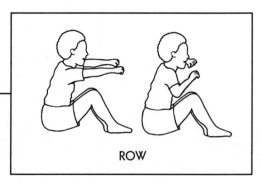

ROW

4. *Move your arms like a ship's sail,*
Being blown about in a stormy gale.
- Reach upward and imagine your arms are sails. ——————

SAIL

5. *Round and round turns*
The steamboat's paddle wheel,
Like a person doing a cartwheel.
- Create large slow circles with your arms. ——————

PADDLE WHEEL

6. *The propeller on a powerboat twists.*
Can you make circles with your wrists?
- Spin your hands and wrists in small circles. ——————

POWER BOAT

STEAMBOAT RACE

INSTRUCTIONS
- Discuss how steamboats often raced up and down the Mississippi River.
- They had to be careful not to crash into logs and sandbars in the river.
- Divide the children into groups of three to five members to create steamboat formations.
- Have the formations stand side by side at one end of the activity area.
- Scatter cones or boxes throughout the activity area.
- On the teacher's command, the groups must walk quickly across the activity area, remaining in formation, without touching a cone or another group.
- Upon reaching the opposite side they travel back "downstream" by moving and paddling in formation.
- If the formations break apart, touch a cone, or collide with another group, they must stop, regroup, and continue forward.
- Recite the following verse while the children complete the race.

Black smoke billows
  As the boilers burn.
Around and around
  The paddle wheels turn.

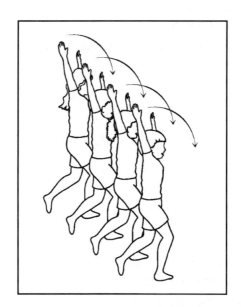

C. WHEELS AND RAILS

Tracks and highways are the trails
Of wheels rolling on asphalt and __ rails.

INTRODUCTION
- Thousands of families traveled West in wagon trains to find new homes.
- It was a long and dangerous trip that took many months.
- Trains, called *locomotives*, were invented to replace the horse and wagon. Steam was used to move the locomotive along rails.
- These powerful steam locomotives helped the USA grow by transporting people and supplies across the country.

WAGON TRAINS

The settlers crossed the Great Plains,
Traveling in wagon trains.

TO THE TUNE:
"DOWN IN THE VALLEY"

INSTRUCTIONS

- Perform the movements while singing the song.

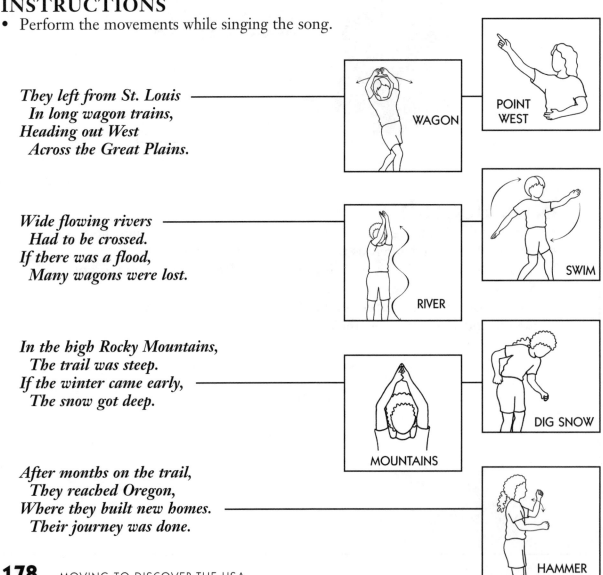

They left from St. Louis
*   In long wagon trains,*
Heading out West
*   Across the Great Plains.*

Wide flowing rivers
*   Had to be crossed.*
If there was a flood,
*   Many wagons were lost.*

In the high Rocky Mountains,
*   The trail was steep.*
If the winter came early,
*   The snow got deep.*

After months on the trail,
*   They reached Oregon,*
Where they built new homes.
*   Their journey was done.*

WAGON   POINT WEST   RIVER   SWIM   MOUNTAINS   DIG SNOW   HAMMER

WAGONS HO!

INSTRUCTIONS

- Divide the children into groups of seven (additional children may be added as oxen to each group). Arrange as shown.
- Use a long jump rope to connect the "Wagon" and "Oxen."
- Have the children act out the verses.

Hitch up the oxen to the wagons;
  It's time to go.
Then call out, "Wagons ho!"

The wagons rock gently
  From side to side.
Across the Great Plains
  The plodding oxen stride.

WAGON TRAIN WITH OXEN

CIRCLED WAGONS

Each night the wagon train
  Forms a circle for protection.
Early the next morning they set out
  Once again in a westerly direction.

The high Rocky Mountains must be crossed.
The wagons follow a steep bumpy trail,
  Side to side, up and down, they are tossed.
- Show me how the wagons bounce on the bumpy trails.

There are many wild rivers the wagons must ford.
Some are deep and swift
  And can wash your supplies overboard!
- What would happen if your wagon tipped over in a swiftly flowing river?

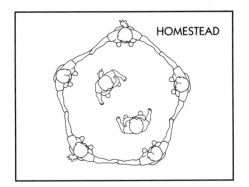

HOMESTEAD

The long trail is finally done.
The way West has been won.
- Use the parts of your wagon to form a fence around the oxen, making a "Homestead."

LAND RUSH

The settlers are eager to begin.
Which wagon do you think will win?

INSTRUCTIONS

- Explain that when new lands became available for homesteading, the government would often conduct a land rush, or race.
- Many settlers formed a long line and raced to claim a new home (land).
- Divide the children into groups of seven to form "Wagons."
- Have the Wagons form a line at one end of the activity area.
- At the teacher's command, the Wagons race across the activity area.
- At the opposite end of the activity area each Wagon forms a "Homestead."

At the starter's command.
They all race to claim a piece of land.

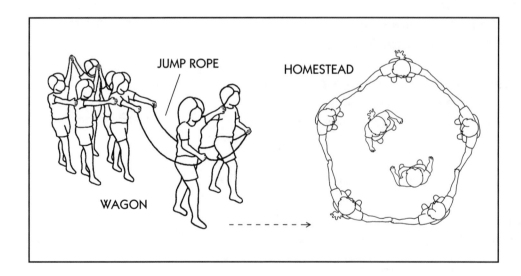

DOWN THE TRACK

MOVING TO THE MUSIC

Cars follow in a long chain,
Down the tracks rolls the train.

TO THE TUNE:
"RAIN, RAIN, GO AWAY"

INSTRUCTIONS

• Encourage the children to perform the movements as they sing.

Train, train, down the track,
Move your arms from front to back.

Woo! Woo! The whistle blows,
Up and down the signal goes.

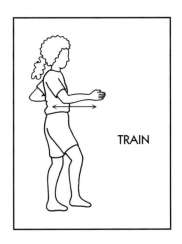
TRAIN

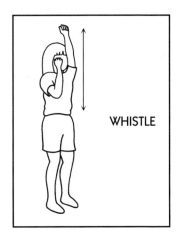
WHISTLE

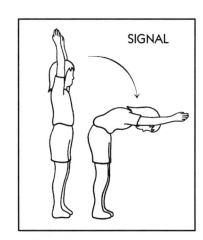
SIGNAL

TOM THUMB'S RACE

The little train lost its race.
The horse and wagon took first place.

The horse and wagon took the day,
But the train was here to stay.

INSTRUCTIONS
- Tom Thumb was the name given to one of the first trains built in the USA. The train's owner challenged a horse and wagon to a race, because he wanted to show that trains could replace horses.
- Divide the children into two groups.
- Group One forms "Trains" with three members standing with their hands on the waist of the person in front of them.
- Group Two creates "Horse and Wagon" formations using three members each.
- The Trains and Wagons race across the activity area.

TRAIN

HORSE & WAGON

MAKE THE CONNECTION

Down the track, the train goes.
At each stop, it adds cars and grows.

INSTRUCTIONS

- Select four "Engines" who stand in each corner of the activity area.
- The remainder of the children scatter throughout the activity area and stand facing different directions. Each "Freight Car" extends both arms forward in preparation to connect with an Engine.
- On the teacher's signal, the Engines begin collecting Freight Cars.
- To do this, an Engine must move past a waiting Car, then back up to connect, at which time, the Car places his or her hands on the Engine's waist.
- This activity continues until all the Cars are connected to one of the Engines.
- The Trains must then circle the activity area three times as quickly as possible and return to the Engine's original start point.
- The object is to be the Train with the greatest number of Cars *and* the first to complete three circuits of the activity area.

The engine must select
The next car, then back up to connect.

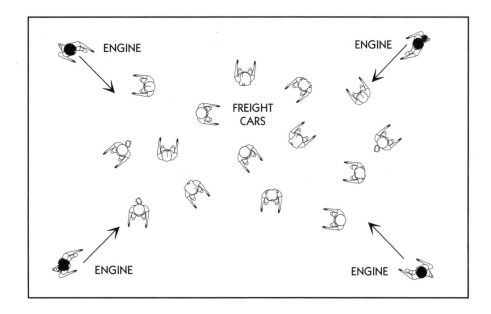

Transportation has changed throughout history
As we have invented new ways to cross the country.

From feet, to boats, to wagons, then trains,
Bicycles, cars, and finally — airplanes.

INTRODUCTION

- The first automobiles were handmade and very costly. It wasn't until 1908 when Henry Ford started to mass produce his Model T that people could afford to purchase cars.
- The newly developed automobile industry created a need for highways and traffic lights.
- A transportation specialist searches for effective means of travel for different groups of people.
- By 1905, Orville and Wilbur Wright had built an airplane that could stay aloft for 30 minutes, creating a new means of travel for America.

INSTRUCTIONS

- This activity challenges the children to identify a variety of different means of travel.
- To begin, select one child to be the "Transportation Specialist" who stands in the center of the activity area. All other children are positioned at one end of the activity area and imitate the movement of one means of transportation.
- On the teacher's signal, the Transportation Specialist shouts a form of transportation. If an individual's item is called, he or she immediately tries to cross to the opposite side without being tagged by the Transportation Specialist.
- If successful, the individual selects a different means of transportation and waits for the new item to be called before crossing again. If the player is tagged, he or she assists the Transportation Specialist in chasing the other players.
- Each time a new means of transportation is called, the teacher adds the item to a large list for all children to view. Play continues until the action has involved a majority of the following forms of transportation.

Automobile	Canoe	Roller skates	Swinging on vines
Airplane	Horse	Running	Tank
Boat	Helicopter	School bus	Train
Blimp	Ice skates	Ship	Trapeze
Bicycle	Jogging	Skateboard	Truck
Camel	Jet	Submarine	Trolley car
Elevator	Limousine	Skis	Van
Escalator	Parachute	Surfboard	Wagon
Glider	Rocket		

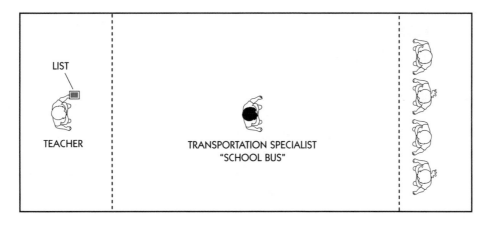

LIST

TEACHER

TRANSPORTATION SPECIALIST
"SCHOOL BUS"

THE MODEL T

It was built so everyone could own a car.
It made Henry Ford a star.

TO THE TUNE:
"TAKE ME OUT TO THE BALLPARK"

INSTRUCTIONS

- Inform the children that the first cars used wooden wagon wheels.
- Ask the children to sing and perform the movements used in starting Henry Ford's Model T.

Crank the motor to start it.
Crank it round and around.
Hop in quick and away you go.
It's not too pretty, and it's kind of slow.
And it's crank, crank, crank on the Model T.
If it won't start, it's a shame.
Cause it's one, two, three cranks it starts,
That's the old Model T.

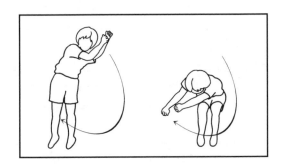

THE WRIGHT BROTHERS

They were the first to fly
An airplane through the sky.

When the American Flyer took flight,
It made heroes of Orville and Wilbur Wright.

INSTRUCTIONS

- Convey that the first flight lasted only 12 seconds and traveled 36 meters (120 feet).
- The longest flight on the first day lasted 59 seconds and traveled 250 meters (852 feet).
- Mark the distance of the Wright brothers' first flight on your activity area with cones.
- Design imaginary American Flyer formations and recreate the first airplane flights (see diagram).

White lines guide the way
As you drive along the winding highway.

Don't cross yellow lines.
Watch for red lights, green lights,
And stop signs.

INSTRUCTIONS

- Tell the children that the first highways across the USA were footpaths created by the American Indians.
- These footpaths became roads and trails for the horses and wagons of the pioneers. Today, highways crisscross the entire country.
- Challenge the children to use floor markers to create a long, twisting highway.
- All children then demonstrate a variety of traveling skills while moving down the winding pathway.

TRAFFIC LIGHTS

INSTRUCTIONS

- Encourage the children to demonstrate the following movements.

Make-believe you are a traffic light,
  Signaling stop and go.
Make a circle with your arms,
  And move them from high to low.
Stop for red on top,
  In the center is yellow; get ready to go,
Take off with green shining down below.

FREQUENT FLIERS

Airlines fly people between cities every day.
Some fly round-trip, others one-way.

INSTRUCTIONS

- Place floor markers to identify different cities around the country.
- Have the children select a partner and create an "Airplane" by placing one hand across each partner's shoulder.
- Make copies of the tickets (see page 189) and give each Airplane a set of tickets.
- Have each Airplane begin its trip at a different city.
- The Airplane must fly to each airport and leave the ticket at the correct location.
- Only one Airplane can take off or land at a time.
- If there is another Airplane at the airport, they must circle the city until the other Airplane has departed.

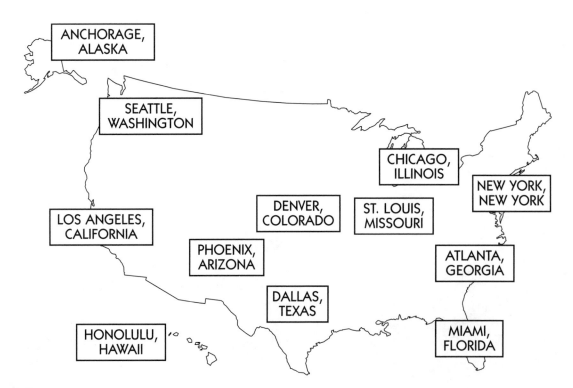

ANCHORAGE, ALASKA

SEATTLE, WASHINGTON

CHICAGO, ILLINOIS

NEW YORK, NEW YORK

LOS ANGELES, CALIFORNIA

DENVER, COLORADO

ST. LOUIS, MISSOURI

PHOENIX, ARIZONA

ATLANTA, GEORGIA

DALLAS, TEXAS

HONOLULU, HAWAII

MIAMI, FLORIDA

TICKET	Seattle, Washington	TICKET	Los Angeles, California
TICKET	New York, New York	TICKET	Miami, Florida
TICKET	Chicago, Illinois	TICKET	Dallas, Texas
TICKET	Denver, Colorado	TICKET	Phoenix, Arizona
TICKET	Honolulu, Hawaii	TICKET	St. Louis, Missouri
TICKET	Anchorage, Alaska	TICKET	Atlanta, Georgia

SAMPLE MOVEMENT DICTIONARY

ADVANCE: To move forward or ahead. When advancing into a street, always look both ways first.

ARCH: To form a curved structure. The tunnel arched overhead.

BALANCE: To be in a steady, stable position. The child balanced on one leg.

BEND: To become curved or crooked. You can bend your knees, legs, or at the tummy.

BOB: To move up and down quickly. The boat bobbed in the water.

BOUNCE: To spring upward after hitting the surface. The ball bounced high in the air.

BURST: To break open suddenly and violently. The balloon burst into small pieces.

CHARGE: To rush at with force. The soldiers charged up the hill.

CLAP: To strike both hands together noisily and quickly. We clapped after the song ended.

CLIMB: To move upward using both the hands and the feet. We climbed to the top of the mountain.

COLLAPSE: To fall down suddenly, or cave in. The tent collapsed to the ground.

CRAWL: To move slowly with arms, hands, knees, belly, and legs along the floor. The baby crawled across the room.

CRUMBLE: To break or fall into small pieces. The wall crumbled to the ground.

CURL: To move in a round shape. The dog curled up into a little ball.

DART: To move suddenly and swiftly in short, quick movements. The police officer darted down the street.

DASH: To move with sudden speed. We dashed through the door and ran upstairs.

DEFLATE: To collapse by letting air out. We deflated the beach ball.

DODGE: To avoid by moving quickly from side to side. The children dodged the snowballs.

DUCK: To lower the head or body quickly. We ducked when we walked through the low doorway.

EXPAND: To become larger. The balloon expanded as the boy inflated it.

FLUTTER: To flap the wings quickly, but not move. The trapped butterfly fluttered its wings.

FLY: To move through the air with wings. Airplanes fly high above the clouds.

FREEZE: To become motionless or fixed. In winter, the water freezes in the lake.

GALLOP: To move by stepping forward with one foot and sliding the other foot to it. The horse galloped across the finish line.

GRAB: To seize suddenly, snatch. The monkey grabbed the bananas.

HOLD: To keep in the arms or hands. Hold the ball tightly in your arms.

HOP: To move up and down or forward on one foot. The children hopped down the long path.

INFLATE: To expand by filling with air. We inflated the balloons.

JERK: To move or pull at with sudden, sharp movements. They jerked the kite from the tree.

JUMP: To take off with both feet, and land on two feet. We jumped over the puddle.

KNEEL: To get down on a bent knee. The soldiers kneeled in front of the king.

LEAN: To support one's weight in a slanted upward position. We leaned against the wall.

LEAP: To stretch one leg forward and land on that foot. The horse leaped over the fence.

LIE DOWN: To be in a flat, resting position. They lowered their bodies to lie down.

LIFT: To raise upward. We lifted the box off the floor.

MARCH: To walk with regular, long, even steps. The soldiers marched in the parade.

MELT: To lessen or fade away gradually, dissolve. The candle melted as it burned.

POUNCE: To jump down upon. The cat pounced on the ball of yarn.

PULL: To tug toward oneself. We pulled the door open.

PUSH: To press away from oneself. We pushed the door open.

REACH: To stretch out or extend upward. I reached for my favorite toy.

RISE: To get up from a lying, sitting, or kneeling position. The sun rises in the morning.

ROLL: To turn over and over. I rolled the ball at the pins.

RUN:	To move quickly by pushing off with the front part of both feet. We ran across the field.
SCAMPER:	To move very quickly with small steps. The squirrels scampered into the forest.
SCATTER:	To separate and go in many directions. The wind scattered the seeds.
SCUFF:	To scrape or drag the feet. We scuffed our feet in the dirt.
SCURRY:	To move lightly and quickly. The little bug scurried past us.
SEARCH:	To look for an object, person, or thing. We searched for sea shells.
SHAKE:	To move with short, quick movements. The monkeys shake the trees to get bananas.
SHIVER:	To shake the whole body out of control. We shivered because of the cold, chilling temperature.
SHRINK:	To decrease in size. The sponge began to shrink into a small shape as it dried.
SHUDDER:	To tremble or shiver suddenly. We shuddered when the teacher scratched the blackboard.
SHUFFLE:	To walk using small steps, keeping the feet and knees together. The basketball player shuffled down the court.
SINK:	To move to a low level. The boat began to sink into the ocean.
SKATE:	To glide along ice. The children skated on the hockey rink.
SKIP:	To step on the toes of one foot and take a small hop on that same foot, followed by a step-hop action on the other foot. The children skipped merrily along down a narrow pathway.
SLIDE:	To move one foot to the side and quickly move the other foot to it. We slid across the ice.
SLITHER:	To move along by gliding. The snake slithered across the sand.
SNEAK:	To move in a sly or secret way. The children sneaked into the kitchen to look for cookies.
SOAR:	To rise, fly, or glide high in the air. The eagle soared through the air.
SPIN:	To rotate at a high speed. I can spin like a top.
SQUEEZE:	To press together with force. We squeezed each other's hands.
STAMP:	To put one foot down heavily and noisily. We stamped to the music.
STAND:	To stay in an upright position. The soldiers needed to stand at attention.
STRETCH:	To become a greater length or width. I stretched my body like a rubber band.
STROLL:	To walk in a slow, relaxed way. We strolled through the park.
STRUT:	To walk in a swaggering or proud manner. We strutted onto the baseball field.
SURROUND:	To encircle. The thief was surrounded by the guards; he couldn't escape.
SWAY:	To move upper body back and forth. The wind made the trees sway.
SWIM:	To move through water using the whole body. The fish were swimming through the water.
TIPTOE:	To walk softly on the tips of the toes. The dancer tiptoed across the stage.
TOPPLE:	To fall over. The blocks toppled over.
TRAMP:	To walk with a heavy step. We tramped up the stairs.
TREMBLE:	To shake from fear or cold. We were so scared that we started to tremble.
TRUDGE:	To walk slowly, or with effort. We trudged through the deep grass.
TUG:	To pull strongly. Each side tugged on the rope.
TURN:	To move around a center, rotate. I turned around and around.
TWIST:	To move the neck, shoulder, hip, or wrist around its own axis. I can twist my wrist to create a circle.
VIBRATE:	To move back and forth quickly. The strings on a guitar vibrate when plucked.
WADDLE:	To sway from side to side using short steps. The duck waddle to the pond.
WALK:	To move the body by stepping forward. We walked to the store.
WANDER:	To move without a destination or purpose. We wandered through the park.
WHIRL:	To spin quickly. The snow whirled around the travelers.
WIGGLE:	To move parts of or the whole body in a swaying motion. The children wiggled their arms and legs.
WOBBLE:	To move from side to side in a shaky manner. The baby began to wobble after standing upright.

A C T I V I T Y   I N D E X

This index identifies five categories to assist readers in locating activities to fit their specific needs. Each **Theme Page** is displayed in bold lettering followed by the name of the activity(ies) related to that theme. The Nature of Activity (i.e., game, rhythm, or action rhyme) is included. Space requirements are conveyed by either an ■ icon representing limited space and less vigorous movement or an □ icon to suggest that ample space is required for full (vigorous movement) participation. The final two categories include recommended equipment and the specific page number of each activity.

A C T I V I T Y   I N D E X

NAME OF ACTIVITY/THEME	NATURE OF ACTIVITY/THEME	SPACE REQUIRED	RECOMMENDED EQUIPMENT	PAGE NUMBER
C. One Land				45
North, South, East, West: Across the USA	Action rhyme	☐	Compass, signs	46
Geographic Regions	Game	☐	None	47
Where In the World Is the USA?	Game	☐	Compass, cones or floor markers	48
"This Land Is Your Land"	Rhythm	■	None	50
SECTION THREE: FAMOUS AMERICANS				
A. George Washington				52
Crossing the Delaware	Game	☐	None	53
B. Paul Revere				54
He'll Be Leaving Boston When He Rides	Rhythm	■	None	55
The Midnight Ride	Game	☐	None	56
Riding to Concord	Game	☐	None	57
Paul Revere's Ride	Game	☐	Floor markers or cones	58
C. Johnny Appleseed				59
Johnny Had an Apple Seed	Rhythm	■	None	60
Apple Tree Tag	Game	☐	None	61
D. Harriet Tubman				62
The Underground Railroad	Game	☐	Floor markers or cones, signs	63
Escape to a Safe House	Game	☐	None	64
E. Noah Webster				65
Movement Dictionary	Game	☐	Sample Movement Dictionary (pg. 190)	66
Spelling Hop	Game	☐	Classroom spelling list	67
F. Susan B. Anthony				68
Have You Ever Heard of Susan B. Anthony?	Rhythm	■	None	69
Tug-of-War Vote	Game	☐	Long, soft rope	70
G. Dr. Martin Luther King Jr.				71
Words to Live By	Game	■	Sign	72
H. Legends of Folklore				73
Rip Van Winkle's Long Sleep	Action rhyme	■	None	74
Pecos Bill's Tornado Ride	Action rhyme	☐	None	75
Catch a Twister	Game	☐	1 hoop	76
John Henry's Famous Race	Action rhyme	■	None	77
Twirling Hammers	Action rhyme	☐	None	78
Hammer Swing	Action rhyme	☐	None	79
Hammer Race	Action rhyme	☐	None	80
SECTION FOUR: NATIVE AMERICANS				
A. American Indian Traditional Games				82
Where the Buffalo Roam	Game	☐	None	83
"You're It" Navajo Game	Game	☐	None	84
Whirling Circles	Game	☐	4 cones or cardboard boxes	85
Fish Trap	Game	☐	None	86
B. Native American Homes				87
Tepee Village	Game	☐	1 sheet per group	88
The Mighty Buffalo Hide	Game	☐	1 sheet per group	89
Longhouse	Game	☐	1 sheet per group	90
Moving the Village	Game	☐	1 sheet per group	91
The Igloo	Game	■	None	92
C. Powwow				93
Special Dances	Action rhyme	■	None	94
Personal Dances	Action rhyme	■	Recorded music, paper, pencils	94

NAME OF ACTIVITY/THEME	NATURE OF ACTIVITY/THEME	SPACE REQUIRED	RECOMMENDED EQUIPMENT	PAGE NUMBER
Fencing the Great Plains	Game	☐	None	139
Jump the Fence	Game	☐	2-by-4 inch planks, cones, or jump ropes	140
E. The Everglades				141
The Everglades Environment	Action rhyme	☐	None	142
Down in the Everglades	Rhythm	■	None	144
SECTION SEVEN: BUILDING A COUNTRY				
A. Communication				146
Spread the Word	Action rhyme	☐	None	147
Body Language	Game	☐	Chart	148
The Pony Express	Game	☐	Floor markers or cones	149
B. Cowpokes				150
Ride 'Em Cowpokes	Game	☐	1 jump rope per pair	151
Roundup	Game	☐	Western music	152
The Trail Drive	Game	☐	None	153
C. Miners				154
Where, Oh Where, Does the Gold Hide?	Rhythm	■	None	155
Claim Jumpers	Game	☐	20 – 24 beanbags; chalk, cones, or tape	156
Gold Nugget Chase	Game	☐	1 pebble or marble per group	157
D. Logging				158
Lumberjacks	Action rhyme	■	None	159
Chop, Chop, Chop the Trees	Rhythm	■	None	160
Our Superhuman Muscles	Action rhyme	■	None	161
E. Agriculture				162
The History of Farming	Action rhyme	■	None	163
Growing Foods	Action rhyme	■	None	164
Crows in the Garden	Game	☐	4 – 6 beanbags, cones or chalk	165
Giving Back to the Land	Game	☐	3 trash cans, sheets of scrap paper	166
SECTION EIGHT: TRANSPORTATION				
A. Momentous Movement				168
Body Moves	Action rhyme	☐	None	169
Moving Through Time	Action rhyme	☐	None	170
B. Boats and Ships				172
Paddle Wheel Steamboat	Action rhyme	■	None	173
Take a Trip on a Ship	Action rhyme	■	None	174
Steamboat Race	Game	☐	8 – 10 cones or boxes	176
C. Wheels and Rails				177
Wagon Trains	Rhythm	■	None	178
Wagons Ho!	Game	☐	1 jump rope per group	179
Land Rush	Game	☐	1 jump rope per group	180
Down the Track	Rhythm	■	None	181
Tom Thumb's Race	Game	☐	None	182
Make the Connection	Game	☐	None	183
D. Means of Travel				184
Transportation Specialist	Game	☐	Poster paper, felt tip marker	185
The Model T	Rhythm	■	None	186
The Wright Brothers	Game	☐	Measuring tape, cones	186
Highways	Game	☐	Floor markers or cones	187
Traffic Lights	Action rhyme	■	None	187
Frequent Fliers	Game	☐	Floor markers or cones, copies of tickets (pg. 189)	188

BIBLIOGRAPHY

Adams, S.H. 1950. *The Pony Express.* New York: Random House.

Altman, S. 1989. *Extraordinary black Americans: From colonial to contemporary times.* Chicago: Children's Press.

Anderson, J. 1984. *The first Thanksgiving feast.* New York: Clarion Books.

Ayer, E. 1992. *Our national monuments.* Brookfield, CT: Millbrook.

Behrens, J. 1986. *Miss Liberty: First lady of the world.* Chicago: Children's Press.

Brookhiser, R. 1996. *Founding father: Rediscovering George Washington.* New York: Free Press.

Brownell, D. 1995. *Heroes of the American Revolution.* Santa Barbara, CA: Bellerophon Books.

Burns, B. 1992. *Harriet Tubman.* New York: Chelsea Juniors.

Demuth, P. 1996. *Johnny Appleseed.* New York: Grosset & Dunlap.

Duncan, D. 1996. *The West: An illustrated history for children.* Boston: Little, Brown.

Fisher, D.H. 1994. *Paul Revere's ride.* New York: Oxford University Press.

Gintzler, A.S. 1994. *Rough and ready loggers: True tales of the Wild West.* Santa Fe, NM: John Muir Publications.

Guzzetti, P. 1996. *The White House.* Parsippany, NJ: Dillon Press.

Harrison J., and E. Van Zandt. 1992. *The young people's atlas of the United States.* New York: Kingfisher Books.

Hirsch Jr., E.D. 1990. *What your second grader needs to know.* New York: Doubleday.

——. 1991. *What your third grader needs to know.* New York: Doubleday.

Howarth, S. 1995. *The children's atlas of the 20th century.* Brookfield, CT: Millbrook.

Johnson, W.W. 1974. *The Forty-Niners*. Alexandria, VA: TimeLife Books.

Kuklin, S. 1996. *Fireworks*. New York: Hyperion Books for Children.

Landau, E. 1990. *Cowboys*. New York: Frankling Watts.

McGovern, A. 1992. *If you lived in colonial times*. New York: Scholastic.

Miller, N. 1992. *The Statue of Liberty*. Danbury, CT: Children's Press.

Prolman, M. 1995. *The Constitution*. Chicago: Children's Press.

Provensen, A. 1995. *My fellow Americans*. San Diego: Harcourt Brace.

Rickman, D. 1985. *Cowboys of the Old West*. New York: Dover.

Ringgold, F. 1992. *Aunt Harriet's underground railroad in the sky*. New York: Crown.

Roop, P., and C. Roop. 1985. *Keep the lights burning, Abbie*. Minneapolis, MN: Carolrhoda.

Shapiro, W.E. 1994. *The Kingfisher young people's encyclopedia of the United States*. New York: Laroussee Kingfisher Chambers.

Sonneborn, L. 1992. *The Cheyenne Indians*. New York: Chelsea House.

Stein, R.C. 1995a. *The California gold rush*. Chicago: Children's Press.

____. 1995b. *The powers of Congress*. Chicago: Children's Press.

Van Leeuwen, J. 1994. *Bound for Oregon*. New York: Dial Books for Young Readers.

Wherry, J.H. 1974. *The totem pole Indians*. New York: Crowell.

York, C.B. 1980. *Johnny Appleseed*. Mahwah, NJ: Troll Associates.

Mike Lee is an artist and creative writer who has dedicated his talents to early childhood fitness since 1986. He is the managing partner of Small World Press in Bayview, Idaho, and the author of *Kids' Animal Exercise Fun.*

Mike has contributed to projects for the New York Department of Human Services and Children's Television Workshop/Sesame Street in New York City. He has presented topics reflecting integrated learning at two national early childhood conferences as well as performed workshops on movement and fitness for children.

A practitioner of independent scholarship and lifelong learning, he is currently working on programs to integrate technology and movement education. In addition to publishing, he consults on computers and environmental design. He can be contacted at child_play@usa.net.

Rhonda L. Clements, Ed.D., is an Associate Professor of Education and Coordinator of Graduate Physical Education at Hofstra University in Hempstead, New York.

Dr. Clements is a consultant in the area of movement for preschool through grade six for several large agencies and corporations as well as local schools throughout New York state.

Dr. Clements is the author of four books on movement and game activities. She received the 1993 Early Childhood News Directors Choice Award for the book, *Let's Move, Let's Play: Developmentally Appropriate Movement and Classroom Activities for Preschool Children.*

The President of the American Association For the Child's Right to Play, Clements also is a member of the American Alliance for Health, Physical Education, Recreation and Dance and the National Association for the Education of the Young Child.